THE SAVVY EDTECH LEADER

Innovative Strategies to Boost Influence and Elevate Your Career

SHERYL ABSHIRE • DIANE DOERSCH • FRANKIE JACKSON • DONNA WILLIAMSON

International Society for Technology in Education
ARLINGTON, VA

The Savvy Edtech Leader
Innovative Strategies to Boost Influence and Elevate Your Career
Sheryl Abshire, Diane Doersch, Frankie Jackson and Donna Williamson

Senior Acquisitions Editor: *Valerie Witte*
Copy Editor: *Courtney Burkholder*
Proofreader: *Joanna Szabo*
Indexer: *Valerie Haynes Perry*
Book Design and Production: *Kim McGovern*
Cover Design: *Edwin Ouellette*

Library of Congress Cataloging-in-Publication Data
Names: Abshire, Sheryl, author. | Jackson, Frankie, author. | Williamson,
   Donna, author. | Doersch, Diane, author.
Title: The savvy edtech leader / innovative strategies to boost influence
   and elevate your career / Sheryl Abshire, Frankie Jackson, Donna
   Williamson, Diane Doersch.
Description: First edition. | Arlington, VA : International Society for
   Technology in Education, [2024] | Includes bibliographical references
   and index.
Identifiers: LCCN 2024025124 | ISBN 9798888370445 (paperback) | ISBN
   9798888370421 (epub) | ISBN 9798888370438 (pdf)
Subjects: LCSH: Educational technology—Study and teaching. | Career
   development. | Educational leadership. | Technological innovations.
Classification: LCC LB1028.3 .A27 2024 | DDC 371.33/4—dc 23/20240608
LC record available at https://lccn.loc.gov/2024025124

First Edition
ISBN: 979-8-88837-044-5

Ebook version available

Printed in the United States of America

ISTE® is a registered trademark of the International Society for Technology in Education.

About ISTE

The International Society for Technology in Education (ISTE) is a nonprofit that brings together a passionate community of global educators. Our vision is that all students engage in transformative learning experiences that spark their imagination and prepare them to thrive in learning and life. ISTE's mission is to empower educators to reimagine and redesign learning through impactful pedagogy and meaningful technology use. We achieve this by offering transformative professional learning, fostering vibrant communities, and ensuring that digital tools and experiences are accessible and effective.

Related ISTE Titles

Education Reimagined: Leading Systemwide Change with the ISTE Standards
   By Helen Crompton

The Technology Coordinator's Handbook, Fourth Edition: A Guide for Edtech Facilitators and Leaders
   By Max Frazier and Doug Hearrington

Elevate Equity in Edtech: Expanding Inclusive Leadership Through the ISTE Standards
   By Victoria Thompson

To see all books available from ISTE, please visit iste.org/books.

About the Authors

 **Dr. Sheryl R. Abshire** is a distinguished educator and visionary leader with an impactful career at the intersection of education and technology. Holding a Ph.D. in Educational Administration and Leadership, she has served as a teacher, librarian, principal, university assistant professor, and CTO for the awarding-winning Calcasieu Parish Public Schools. Her leadership has been instrumental in integrating technology into education, and she played a pivotal role in establishing the ISTE National Education Technology Standards and contributing to the U.S. DOE National Educational Technology Plan.

Abshire is an ISTE Certified Educator and a Certified Cybersecurity Rubric Evaluator (CCRE). She has held significant positions, including serving as Consortium for School Networking (CoSN) Chair of the Board from 2005–2009, President of the Louisiana Association of Computer Using Educators (LACUE), and Founder and Chair of CoSN's Louisiana Chief Technology Officers' Association (LA-CTO). Additionally, she was appointed to the USAC Board by the FCC to represent schools and libraries on E-Rate matters. Her contributions have been recognized with numerous awards, including the CoSN Seymour Papert Lifetime Achievement Award, ISTE Making It Happen Award, and the Lifetime Achievement Award from the Learning Counsel. Additionally, she was the first teacher inducted into the National Teachers Hall of Fame and honored by President Bill Clinton and Secretary of Education Richard Riley at the White House.

Her influence extends globally through her presentations at major conferences and leadership on various boards. Abshire has also been acknowledged as one of the Top 100 EdTech Influencers by *EdTech Digest*. She is a prolific author, with extensive publications on grant writing, educational technology, personalized learning, cybersecurity, IT integration, and issues related to diversity, equity, and inclusion.

Abshire continues to be a fierce advocate for education, frequently testifying before Congress and the FCC; and serving on the CoSN Policy Committee, the ISTE Policy Committee, the CoSN Driving K–12 Innovation Board, and as a facilitator for the CoSN Early Career K–12 CTO Academy.

 **Diane Doersch** is the Senior Director of Information Technology at Digital Promise, where she spearheads initiatives that drive innovation in education advancing the use of technology. With a wealth of experience, Doersch previously served as the Chief Technology and Information Officer for the Green Bay Area Public Schools, where she was instrumental in integrating advanced technological solutions to enhance educational outcomes. She holds a master's degree in educational technology from Lesley University and a Certified Education Technology Leader (CETL) National Certificate from the Consortium for School Networking (CoSN). She is a Certified Cybersecurity Rubric Evaluator (CCRE), showcasing her expertise in ensuring the security and integrity of educational technology systems. As a trailblazer in the field, she was a founding member and former president of the WISEdash Local Consortium, a coalition of Wisconsin school districts dedicated to creating a robust data warehouse for enhanced educational insights and decision-making.

From 2021 to 2024, Doersch served as the President of Northeast Wisconsin Women in Technology (WIT), an organization passionately committed to attracting, educating, and supporting women in the technology sector. Her leadership extends nationally as she serves as the Chair of CoSN from 2023 to 2025, guiding the organization's board of directors and championing the advancement of educational technology across the country. Doersch is also a sought-after speaker and thought leader, frequently presenting at national conferences and contributing to various publications on the future of educational technology.

Doersch's career also included directing technology for the Verizon Innovative Learning Schools program, which focuses on providing under-resourced schools with the technology and support needed to ensure digital equity. Her work emphasizes dismantling inequitable systems and providing all students with the resources necessary to succeed in a digital world. Her dynamic leadership and visionary approach continue to inspire and influence the educational technology landscape.

 **Frankie Jackson** is a nationally recognized Chief Technology Officer (CTO) with over 30 years of experience leading education technology initiatives at the state and national levels. She has worked in large school districts with 25,000 to 130,000 students. Throughout her career, Jackson has demonstrated a unique blend of technical expertise and leadership skills, often integrating performance excellence frameworks such as quality management and service methodologies.

Jackson is a Certified Education Technology Leader (CETL) from the CoSN and a Certified Cybersecurity Rubric Evaluator (CCRE). She serves on the Consortium for School Networking's (CoSN) Policy Committee, Advanced Professional Learning Committee, Cybersecurity Advisory, and Driving K–12 Innovation Board. As the project lead for the national Cybersecurity Coalition for Education, Jackson is instrumental in certifying education leaders as cybersecurity evaluators. She also designs and instructs content for CoSN's Certified Education Technology Leader (CETL) project management course.

Jackson's dedication to the field is further evidenced by her numerous accolades, including being named to the International Chief Technology Officer (CTO) Women in Information Technology Top 10 List, receiving the Chief Technology Officer (CTO) of the Year honors from CoSN, and receiving a twice-recognized Texas Educational Technology Leaders (TETL) Grace Hopper Award.

Additionally, Jackson is an independent consultant and technical advisor, contributing to various educational technology projects and initiatives. She is passionate about mentoring and coaching the next generation of education technology leaders, and she frequently speaks at national and state conferences on topics such as innovation, edtech leadership, and cybersecurity.

Jackson's educational background includes a master's degree in instructional technology and various other degrees and certifications, including the National Institute of Standards and Technology (NIST) Cybersecurity Practitioner certification. She also holds certifications as a John Maxwell coach and mentor, emphasizing her commitment to both technical and soft skills development in the education sector.

**Donna Williamson** has made a significant impact in the field of educational technology with her extensive experience and numerous leadership roles. Beginning her career as a technology leader and teacher, she later served as the Technology Director (CTO) for Mountain Brook Schools. At Mountain Brook, she led the district's technology initiatives and managed all operational and instructional technology resources, culminating in the district being recognized as ISTE's 2016 Distinguished District.

Williamson has been deeply involved with the Consortium for School Networking (CoSN), serving as a board member and as the chairperson of CoSN Alabama Leaders. She is the Project Director for the CoSN Early Career K–12 CTO Academy, where she mentors new and aspiring CTOs in the education sector. Her role as a frequent speaker at national and state conferences allows her to present on various topics, including innovation, edtech leadership, communication, soft skills in edtech, and data analytics.

Her excellence in the field has been recognized with numerous awards, such as the ISTE Making It Happen Award, the Alabama Educational Technology Association Sally Moore Award, the National Withrow CTO Award for Educators Honorable Mention, and *EdTech Digest's* Trendsetter Award. Additionally, she has been listed among the Top 100 Influencers in EdTech by *EdTech Digest*.

Williamson has obtained several certifications, including Certified Cybersecurity Rubric Evaluator (CCRE). Additionally, she has published about cybersecurity insurance and has written various state and national technology plans and technology education curriculums. She also produced a series of how-to videos, further showcasing her dedication to sharing knowledge and best practices in educational technology. She is a frequent contributor to various educational publications, continuing to influence the edtech community with her insights and expertise. Williamson's dedication and contributions to educational technology make her a prominent figure in the field, inspiring future generations of edtech leaders.

Publisher Acknowledgments

ISTE gratefully acknowledges the contributions of the following:

ISTE Standards Reviewers

Ruth Okoye

Tiffany Rexhausen

Manuscript Reviewers

Ronda Blevins

Cammie Kannekens

Laura Thomas

Dedication

This book is dedicated to all the educators who have profoundly influenced, steadfastly supported, and consistently promoted us throughout our careers. Your passion for education and unwavering commitment to excellence have illuminated our paths, inspiring us to strive for greatness and to innovate within the realm of educational technology.

To the countless Edtech Leaders who have generously shared their expertise and talents, we owe you a debt of gratitude. Your collaboration, innovation, and willingness to push boundaries have been instrumental in shaping our journey. Your insights and dedication have not only enriched our understanding but have also propelled the entire field of educational technology forward.

And to our incredibly supportive families, thank you for your unwavering encouragement, patience, and love. Your belief in us has been the foundation upon which we've built our careers and pursued our dreams. Your sacrifices and understanding have made this journey possible, and for that, we are eternally grateful.

—*Sheryl Abshire, Diane Doersch, Frankie Jackson, and Donna Williamson*

Contents

Contents

Foreword

Writing the foreword to this remarkable book of wisdom for Edtech Leaders is both a true honor and a bit intimidating. It is an honor because I have known all four authors for decades, and I consider them not only my colleagues but also my friends. Their collective expertise and experience in the field of educational technology are unparalleled.

In the introduction to *The Savvy Edtech Leader*, the authors mention they have more than 120 years of combined experience. I can vouch for this claim, having witnessed their savvy leadership during my three decades of leading CoSN, the professional Edtech Leadership association. They might even be underestimating their combined wisdom and being modest in their calculations.

It is also intimidating because these authors set the highest expectations for themselves and their professional edtech colleagues. When they ask you to engage and comment, they genuinely expect you to be insightful and astute. I will certainly give it my best.

My advice to all Edtech Leaders is simple: Read this book. The combined wisdom within these pages is clear and practical, and it challenges you to excel. Most importantly, while providing valuable tips for your leadership, the authors consistently emphasize that success is a team effort. This reminds me of Michelle Obama's quote, "Success is not about climbing to the top; it's about lifting others as you climb."

These four accomplished female leaders embody the advice they generously share. They have all played significant roles in their respective school districts and provided national leadership that has shaped education and technology in education over the years. They have defined the gold standard for Edtech Leadership and have generously mentored the next generation.

From the early days of computers and the internet, these visionaries have helped shape the growing field of edtech. They truly are Savvy Edtech Leaders. Any one of them could have authored a book on leadership. However, we are particularly fortunate that they have collaborated to create this comprehensive guide for today's and tomorrow's Edtech Leaders.

— *Keith Krueger, CEO, Consortium for School Networking (CoSN)*

Introduction

In today's rapidly evolving educational landscape, district-level technology leaders in K–12 institutions are indispensable. As guardians of cybersecurity, data privacy, procurement, network systems, and professional development, savvy Edtech Leaders shoulder the responsibility of navigating complex laws and regulations while spearheading innovation within budgetary constraints. This book provides critical leadership strategies that will assist you, the tech-savvy leader, in boosting your influence and elevating your career.

Despite the critical nature of these positions, a standardized universal nomenclature and responsibility set for district-level technology leaders remain elusive. ISTE and CoSN have outlined essential skills, designated titles such as chief technology officer, and developed certification programs, yet the variation in Edtech Leader titles persists across districts of differing sizes and locations.

In this book, we use the term "Edtech Leader" to encompass the diverse roles and responsibilities of Edtech Leadership individuals or teams at the district level. Whether managing large departments or operating within small, outsourced structures, Edtech Leaders are the key decision makers entrusted with navigating the convergence of technology and education.

We invite you to embark on a transformative journey with *The Savvy Edtech Leader*, a groundbreaking guide that explores the secrets of successful Edtech Leaders, who not only manage technical intricacies but also master the art of inspiring their teams. The authors provide strategies that acknowledge these leaders' dual roles: adept managers of systems and exemplary leaders of individuals.

Delve into the captivating realm where effective management of *things* converges with the artistry of leading *people*. Have you ever been curious about the alchemy of leadership charisma? Have you ever wondered what makes certain leaders magnetic? What draws people to follow them, not just within their departments but across the broader educational community? This book unravels the mystery, offering keen insights into the charisma, confidence, and communication styles that command attention and support.

The Savvy Edtech Leader isn't just another leadership manual; it's a twelve-chapter odyssey with easily digestible sections, each unveiling specific strategies. Whether you're aspiring to stand out in your organization, seeking career advancement, or striving to navigate the complexities of Edtech Leadership, this book is your compass.

The authors, with a combined expertise of more than 120 years—as chief technology officers, project directors, principals, librarians, teachers, and more—share their wealth of knowledge and extensive experiences spanning the spectrum of educational technology. They provide a comprehensive guide to leadership, vision, strategic planning, foresight, ethics, interpersonal skills, and team building.

 This guide isn't just theoretical; it's a pragmatic companion for your leadership journey. *The Savvy Edtech Leader* is truly a holistic master class in leadership enhancement and excellence; it is aligned with industry standards like CoSN CETL certification, and each chapter includes connections to the ISTE Standards, Education Leaders section. The Education Leaders section of the ISTE Standards supports the implementation of both the Student and Educator sections of ISTE Standards by targeting the knowledge and behaviors required for leaders to empower teachers and boost student learning. This section is focused on equity, digital citizenship, visioneering, team and systems building, continuous improvement and professional growth. Scan the QR code (iste.org/standards/education-leaders) to learn more.

 In addition, scan the QR code (tinyurl.com/34sbdmp3) to access an online Edtech Leadership self-assessment. This interactive tool propels you through a journey of self-improvement, ensuring your leadership skills continuously evolve.

The Savvy Edtech Leader provides comprehensive guidance, drawing upon the collective wisdom of experienced practitioners, to empower Edtech Leaders in meeting the evolving challenges of the digital era. We hope that this resource will catalyze excellence and innovation in Edtech Leadership across diverse K–12 settings.

Are you ready to transcend the challenges of Edtech Leadership and emerge not just as an effective leader but as an exemplary leader of leaders? Join Sheryl, Diane, Frankie, and Donna as they guide you through a transformative journey brimming with leadership strategies that promise not just survival but unparalleled success in the dynamic landscape of Edtech Leadership.

1

Beyond Vision Statements
Realizing Goals through Tenacity and Teamwork

I n today's fast-paced world, organizations require authentic, purpose-driven leadership—leadership that not only casts a vivid vision of the future but is grounded in the present realities and intricacies of an organization's mission. This is where an inspiring purpose becomes paramount. This purpose not only defines the very essence of an organization's mission but also answers the fundamental question: How does the organization position itself for success? For a successful Edtech Leader such an inspiring purpose isn't just about crafting statements. It's about galvanizing the team, ensuring every member recognizes the value of their contributions, and together, striving to bring the organization's vision to fruition.

From sports to problem-solving committees, we've all been part of a team in one capacity or another. The beauty of teamwork lies not just in accomplishing the end goal, but in the journey itself. It's about the camaraderie, the blend of diverse perspectives, and the synergetic energy that propels the team forward. While synergy is critical, at the same time each individual team member must be aware of the unique value they contribute.

THE ISTE STANDARDS

Chapter 1 highlights the critical role of visionary and equitable leadership in educational technology, which resonates with specific ISTE Education Leader Standards. Specifically, the **Equity and Citizenship Advocate Standard (3.1)** emphasizes the importance of using technology to foster inclusivity, digital citizenship, and equitable access to educational resources. Edtech Leaders are encouraged to ensure that all students benefit from skilled teachers and the necessary technology for engaging learning experiences, thereby addressing the diverse needs of every student. This standard supports the chapter's call for leaders who not only envision but actively work towards a more inclusive and equitable educational environment.

The **Visionary Planner Standard (3.2)** requires leaders to engage stakeholders in creating a strategic vision for integrating technology in ways that transform learning. This involves not just the creation of a strategic plan, but also its ongoing evaluation, adjustment, and communication to ensure it remains aligned with educational goals and technological advancements. This standard underscores the introduction's theme of purpose-driven leadership that not only envisions but methodically implements plans to achieve and sustain organizational success.

Paint a Picture of the Future

Nothing can create passion like a vision of what is possible. This vision is one of the most effective ways to fire up your team. A clear vision paints a picture of the organization's desired future with an inspiring purpose.

High-performing leaders develop a clear vision via a deep understanding of their leadership role. Their vision is partially about who they want to become. Their vision embodies the organization's mission, which includes the *why*. It's so compelling that others can't imagine not participating.

The vision also embodies the leader's credibility and influence. What the leader stands for helps make the vision come alive. The vision becomes unified when people believe in the leader and choose to follow, embracing the vision as if it were their own.

Developing a vision involves visualizing what the organization will be like in one, three, or even five (or more) years. It requires imagination. It should be relatable.

 ## *KEY STRATEGIES*

- Think about what you are passionate about. Building your vision is an inside job. You can't borrow another leader's vision.

- Carefully craft your vision with your team in mind. How do you expect others to follow if your ideas aren't clear? Don't expect others to do this for you. You are the leader!

- Be emotional about your vision. Let your vision be the energy that builds the momentum. Get excited first; then others will want to follow.

- Stay on message. Communicate your vision over and over. Find ways to weave part of your vision into every communication.

- Create passion throughout. Passion is contagious. Passion is energy.

Passion Gets the Heart Pumping

Start with your heart. Taking your vision to heart will arouse the emotions needed to keep the momentum going over time.

Crafting the vision is hard work. It requires a concentrated effort on your part. You may want to step away from the office or your surroundings.

Start with a highly ambitious statement. Don't get stuck on the how. Don't get bogged down in the details. The vision isn't the mission. It's not *how you will get there*. The vision is *where you are heading and why*. It is your grand picture of the future.

Write down specific descriptions of what success looks like. Ignore any challenges you foresee. Write in the present tense. The result will be a narrative that may be several pages in length. A condensed version of the vision will be helpful for others, but you, as the leader, need specific details to communicate the vision effectively.

Brilliance Starts with Questions, Not Answers

Consider these four questions:

1. **Who are we in the future?** Imagining the future helps you visualize success. Details bring depth to your vision. For example: We are technology experts that are talented, customer-oriented, and of impeccable character. We are driven and eager to serve K–12 staff and students. Our team works together to ensure we exceed all customer expectations. We are agile, open to change, and able to embrace new technologies quickly.

2. **What technology programs and services will you deliver?** Answering this question helps everyone to understand what we do. People must have a clear idea of the programs and services we imagine. For example: We provide innovative technology solutions. We help educators use technology in a meaningful way. We elevate student success. We deliver world-class technology programs and services.

3. **Whom do we serve?** These are your customers. For example: We serve all students, from pre-kindergarten to twelfth grade. We serve teachers and administrators, who provide service and support to students. We serve support staff, who provide student services. We serve parents and legal guardians of our students.

4. **What impact will you have?** What are the intended effects of your vision? For example: Because of our technological solutions, educators and support staff won't waste a minute of their valuable time. Our students are ready to enter college or the workforce with certifications or specialized knowledge and skills. Students are creative, lifelong learners. Customers are engaged and have all the programs and services they need to be influencers of education technology.

Make the Picture Come Alive

Our vision is who we want to be. A great leader makes their vision come alive for others, so they are inspired to act. Make your vision concrete, specific, and inviting; others will join you in making it a reality. Following are some vision examples:

- The most innovative technology solution provider of K–12 digital solutions in the nation.

- The trusted technology partner who elevates education through innovation.

- World-class, creating the best of the best technology solutions to serve students and educators.

- LEADers through learning, empowerment, achievement, and our dreams.

- The most innovative, responsive, customer-driven technology partner in K–12.

- Seamless and most admired by those we serve.

- World-class, driven by the innovation, teamwork, and creativity of our people.

- Fulfilling student dreams through the experiences of innovative technologies.

- Delighting our students and customers 100%, every time, all the time.

- Enablers of the future through technology innovation.

- The preeminent education technology support team that fully engages our people.

- Making our students' dreams a reality.

- An efficient, world-class education technology system that engages and prepares all students to be globally competitive in college and careers.

- The team that never wastes an instructional second of time due to technology disruption.

- The district that transforms education.

- The team where technology is always on, always fast, always innovative, and always seamless.

- The benchmark for the best education technology in K–12 across the nation.

- The partner of choice for best-in-class education technology services.

- The world leader at connecting students and educators to technology experiences.

- The go-to technology partner for K–12 education.

- Bringing educational technology to the hands of everyone, and always available.

- Connecting students and educators so they are productive, successful, and lifelong learners.

- The fabric of innovative, real-time communication and learning in our school system.

- Helping students and customers have the best possible experience with technology.

- Sparking transformational learning via innovative technologies.

Leaders Are Repeaters

Once your vision is concrete, read it every day. Share it. Build momentum by bringing the vision alive through posters, logos, sheer excitement, or whatever it takes to consistently reinforce the vision. It's not enough to just communicate the vision. You must believe in the vision wholeheartedly.

Make the Dream Work through Teamwork

Are you a part of a team? Chances are the answer is yes. When you think of teams, you may think of sports, service, cross-functional teams with many other department leaders, or problem-solving teams. All those teams should be working toward a common goal. You are an integral part of any team you're on. You can add value and serve others.

 KEY STRATEGIES

- Identify your strengths and offer them to your team. You have much to offer the group, and you have an outstanding opportunity to learn from others on the team.

- Be prepared for team meetings; do your homework. Each meeting should have action items and a list of tasks that team members should do between sessions.

- Be a strong supporter of everyone on the team. Your attention to the needs of the individuals on the team will help make the team stronger.

- Emphasize reflection in the team's work. Take time to highlight the good and uncover the gaps.

What do you appreciate about being on a team? Is it the everyday experiences and camaraderie? Is it the diversity of the team and the way many perspectives are incorporated into the solution? Or is it the way members of the group can energize and bring others forward?

A powerful saying oft attributed to Henry Ford is "If everyone is moving forward together, then success takes care of itself." Teams who move forward together can accomplish so much more. Individual strengths and talents can be maximized, and diversity in thought allows for more inclusive solutions.

What part do you play in the team?

Good team members come prepared to meetings. If you have tasks assigned to you, come to each meeting with your materials ready and accessible. If appropriate, provide opportunities for teammates to access your content ahead of the meeting so they can review it early and use meeting time for clarification or revision of your work.

Working on a team can be difficult due to the many personalities involved. Put the group's needs ahead of your own. If everybody has their own agenda in addition to the group's main goals, progress can get muddied very quickly. Good team members understand the purposes of the team and are "all in" to help meet the goals. Sometimes being a good team member means that you must reprioritize your thinking to accomplish the goal. It doesn't mean you've conceded or are a pushover. It does mean that you've changed your thinking due to new information gained through robust discussion with the team.

Great team members know the value of their teammates and are grateful for the opportunity to work and learn with them. Edtech Leaders see the individual contributions of team members. You should remind each team member why they are part of the team and what they have to offer. When members can easily see the benefits of their and their teammates' contributions, the team can focus on orchestrating the work and figuring out how each person's skill set contributes to the whole.

Each person comes to a team with their own strengths and styles. Is your group good at big ideas but needs somebody to help refine details? Is your group so detailed that it needs prodding to think about the big picture? As an Edtech Leader, you may find yourself helping to fill holes in the group's skill set either with your own skills or even better by encouraging another to take on the gap as a learning opportunity.

All projects have ebbs and flows. A good team member recognizes when the team needs a boost to accelerate the work, or needs to take a break. What are your gifts for energizing your team? Are you a good cheerleader? What has worked for you? How can you energize a team?

Your team members are human. You need to care for their needs. Sometimes, they may work beyond their physical and mental capabilities. Look for signs of mental fatigue, stress, or physical exhaustion. Asking your teammates how they are doing, or noting, "I've observed _____ lately," can open the door to a conversation. Sometimes, your colleagues just need somebody to listen to them as they vent.

Respect for others on the team is essential. If you and another team member disagree, you need to be able to approach your colleague privately and discuss the issue honestly. Airing disputes in front of the team can divide team members. Disparaging team members in front of the group only reflects poorly on you.

Encourage your team to see the value of every team member and share appreciation. Each member should give credit to their teammates and amplify their voices even when they are not in the room.

The best team members do not come from a place of pride or ego. Instead, they have the "everybody wins" mindset. Any team member's win also belongs to the team.

The Art of Self-Reflection

One of the most critical skills of a good team member is the art of self-reflection. Ask yourself:

- What is my part in the work of our team?
- Am I upholding my part of the project?
- Am I communicating enough so the team understands my progress and commitments to the group?
- What can I do to be a better teammate?
- Am I honest and authentic with my team, or are there things I'm holding back? If so, why?
- Am I holding myself accountable for my actions?

A good teammate only takes on part of the group's workload. It's important to hold others accountable as well. A team member might fall behind for any number of reasons. Displaying empathy and coming from a place of care, rather than judgment, is the key to assisting your teammates in getting unstuck.

Possible ways to approach your colleague include:

- How is everything going?
- Can I assist or support you?
- I've noticed that you haven't hit your last goal. I know things have been busy—do you need more clarity?
- I know a deadline is coming soon, and I'm working to finish things. How are things going for you?
- Is there anything that we can do together?

Create and Support Systems for Success

Processes and systems can assist with goal achievement. Perhaps your team could use a formal Agile (tinyurl.com/AgileResourcess) or Kaizen (tinyurl.com/KaizenInfo) methodology to reach an endpoint; other times, the team might benefit from a continuous improvement model that incorporates the steps *plan*, *do*, *study*, and *act*. Building consistency in how you get work done creates a shared expectation for the team. Your good habits set an example and elevate the work of everybody.

Pass the Value On

You now understand many aspects that help your team reach its goals. Your colleagues may take a while to identify that your techniques helped propel the team forward. Your behind-the-scenes role modeling for other team members benefits everyone. At the end of a project, during your debrief, help team members reflect upon the work that went well. This reflection is an excellent opportunity to help solidify successful techniques. On the flip side, identifying what didn't work well and discussing how to mitigate those speed bumps next time helps build continuous improvement.

As your team finds its flow, perhaps some of the tactics you introduced will serve as a blueprint for the future, becoming a system that will serve as the "secret sauce" for your subsequent tasks.

Persist with Consistency

According to *Merriam-Webster*, to be consistent means "marked by harmony, regularity, or steady continuity: free from variation or contradiction." A successful Edtech Leader builds a consistent structure for communications and meetings so that their team members and other departmental leaders know what to expect.

 KEY STRATEGIES

- Document key processes.

- Combine your best thinkers to find solutions. Collaborative groups of subject-matter experts and cross-functional teams benefit the organization.

- Build your meeting schedule and publish it. Creating a consistent schedule of meetings so that information can flow up and down from your management position is a low-energy, high-yield action.

- Prioritize decision-making collaborative time, and make those meetings a priority.

- Build a system for agendas and note-taking, and stick to it. Accurate documentation is essential; this information must be transparent and accessible.

When you are consistent in Edtech Leadership, you keep doing the things you know will work. Your team should know what to expect from you as far as meetings and information sharing. As an Edtech Leader working to build a team culture, you might plan to post weekly with department and team member news, critical reminders for the upcoming week, celebrations, or a list of birthdays to acknowledge. When staff can expect the same behavior on a schedule, it gives them a sense of calm and something on which they can count.

When you create consistency for your team, you create a clear direction for the team. Clarifying where the department is headed allows everybody to see how they fit into goal fulfillment. Your consistency also provides stability to your team. They can anticipate the expectations, decision-making processes, and outcomes. Consistency eliminates uncertainty and allows staff to focus on tasks.

As an Edtech Leader, your methods appropriately assign resources to the right things. Your whole department should be able to assess resource allocation accurately and put funds or work energy into areas that need it most, because they all understand the larger picture.

Routinely emphasizing priority items helps support consistency. An example could be in creating a set schedule of organizational meetings. Leverage face-to-face collaboration time by strictly scheduling key meetings with district teams. Make attendance at these meetings mandatory. Having your team of subject matter experts and decision-makers around the table regularly is essential so that projects can be completed on time.

For example, your departmental leadership team meets on Monday mornings to plan and align the work of your entire department for the upcoming week. Important collaborative decisions are made, and processes with timelines are outlined. To prepare for these Monday meetings, your leaders should build a routine of summarizing key progress notes onto a shared document in the days before the meeting. Updates must be completed by Monday morning's start of the workday so the leadership team members can review them before the weekly leadership meeting begins. Thus, valuable face-to-face time during the Monday meeting is not spent verbally updating colleagues on things that took place in the previous week. Those items can easily be read on a document. If there are questions about the updates, they can be asked at the leader meeting. An agenda for the Monday meeting should be created ahead of time by all the leaders and marked where decisions must be made. Detailed meeting minutes should be taken, and links to key documents should be included. At the end of the meeting, action items are reviewed, and clarity in messaging to the staff is coordinated.

All the leaders in that meeting take the decisions, messaging, and information to their teams to work out the details at their level. The team members ask questions, and the managers hear concerns. Leaders also have their ears to the ground regarding what other departments are experiencing. This vital intelligence should be brought to the Monday meeting to inform the work of the leaders. Each department leader should have regular meetings with the cabinet-level leaders and the top person in charge. Running agendas are created in all meetings, and minutes are taken. All meetings end with a review of the action items and next steps. By building an institutional schedule of meetings that is consistent and transparent, planning and executing projects is more efficient and collaborative.

In contrast, scheduling weekly meetings "on the fly" is a high-energy, low-yield endeavor. It's quite possible that personal schedules could be so filled that important decision-making meetings could take weeks to schedule. Your organization does not have that much time to wait.

Creating a consistent, transparent schedule of meetings promotes timely decision-making. Your scheduled meetings drive accountability and information gathering so that all information is present to make the best-informed decisions possible. The frequency of meetings allows for challenges to be addressed promptly, opportunities to be capitalized upon, and deviations to be discussed as they arise. It allows for collaboration, alignment with organizational goals, and the coordination of work. Having all the decision-makers around the table regularly allows for adjusting resources between departments or teams and reevaluating resource needs.

Regular meetings continually foster accountability among all participants. The expectation that action items are completed by the next meeting so that projects can move forward is required for success. Consistent meetings provide transparency and allow a structured venue to share insights, progress, and information. Clarity is achieved by enabling leaders to provide the rationale for their decisions. Open, regular communication also helps to build trust among team members.

Lastly, your consistent scheduling provides regular decision-making meetings that provide accountability to your upper leadership and Board of Education. Consistent meetings demonstrate that the organization is actively managing and governing its operations. They provide an opportunity to report progress, address concerns, and ensure that decisions align with your district's ethical and legal obligations.

Invest in the Community

There's a proverb that says, "If you want to go quickly, go alone. If you want to go far, go together." Community leaders take responsibility for the well-being and improvement of their communities. An effective leader uses what each community member has to offer to help push the community toward success.

Are you a community leader? Are you interested in becoming one? Are you willing to invest in your community to improve it?

To invest in a community as a leader, you must formulate a clear, compelling personal vision that aligns with the community's needs. This vision should articulate where you see the community heading and how you plan to lead it there.

To communicate this vision, use multiple mediums such as community meetings, social media, and newsletters. Explain how your idea will positively impact everyone involved.

Additionally, you need to consider how you will listen to people in the community. Active listening is a crucial leadership skill. As an effective Edtech Leader, you can implement regular meetings, surveys, and open-door policies to ensure you hear all community members' concerns. Be open to constructive criticism, and ensure you listen, understand, and respond to the concerns.

 ## KEY STRATEGIES

- Devise and share a convincing personal vision that echoes the community's needs.

- Engage in proactive listening to the community through public meetings, questionnaires, and open-door policies.

- Assume responsibility by acknowledging challenges, taking accountability for actions, and championing the community's cause.

- Establish straightforward, achievable objectives that are in harmony with your vision and the requirements of the community.

- Foster growth by identifying and addressing individual needs while promoting group cohesion. Focus on understanding and supporting each community member's unique needs and strengths.

As an Edtech Leader, it's imperative that you think about how you will take responsibility for your community. You must recognize and address problems, be accountable for your actions, and strive for constant improvement. You must also advocate for your community when meeting with external entities. Be proactive in understanding your community's issues and develop plans to address them.

Establishing clear, attainable goals is a vital part of community leadership. These goals should align with your vision and the community's needs. Include short-term and long-term objectives, and regularly assess and adjust these goals as necessary. Make sure to involve community members in the goal-setting process to ensure their buy-in.

How will you serve individuals in the community? Helping individuals requires personalized attention. Acknowledge individual contributions, understand their unique needs, and support them in their personal growth. Regular one-on-one meetings, recognition programs, and opportunities for professional development are all ways to serve individuals in your community.

Another critical consideration includes how you will serve the community as a whole. Look to foster a sense of unity and belonging by promoting teamwork, building shared values, and ensuring a harmonious environment. Providing opportunities for community activities, reinforcing the importance of every member, and working towards collective achievements are also critical.

Furthermore, propose specific changes in how you will lead others. Reflect on your current leadership style and seek feedback from community members to identify areas for improvement. Changes could include increased transparency, better communication, more involvement of community members in decision-making, and new initiatives to meet community needs.

Contemplate how you will get the work done. You should build a strong team; delegate tasks based on individuals' strengths and interests; establish clear roles, responsibilities, and deadlines; and utilize project management tools to track progress and ensure efficient execution of tasks.

Remember, Edtech Leadership is not just about getting the work done yourself but also about motivating and supporting others to do their best work. Recruiting and preparing others in the community to become leaders is a crucial task. Start by identifying potential leaders within the community and on your team—those who are engaged, reliable, and passionate about the community. Provide them with opportunities to lead small projects or tasks to develop their skills. Offer mentoring and coaching, and consider leadership development programs. Share your experiences and lessons learned to guide them on their leadership journey. By creating a pipeline of future leaders, you ensure your community's sustainability and continued growth.

Finally, as an Edtech Leader, investing in your community may be one of your most significant contributions to your organization *and* your community. You may be destined for substantial and meaningful community leadership. The decision to undertake this pivotal role in shaping your surroundings rests solely with you.

Feel empowered to chase your aspirations and engage in work that brings you fulfillment. You possess the potential to effect profound transformations in the lives of those around you. Never underestimate the value of your distinctive contribution to the world.

From Purpose to Practice

Navigating the Edtech Leadership Landscape

To be an effective Edtech Leader, you must start within yourself. What do you think about your work and how you do it? What is your purpose, and how does it show in your career? Is it all harmonious, or is your purpose (your *why*) in disarray? This chapter shares our perspectives on making a name for yourself in educational technology. It also talks about how to lead both when times are good and when they are challenging, requiring you to engage in difficult conversations. Guiding others in their leadership journey is an honor. This chapter provides strategies you can implement to help your staff become functional members of your team as well as leaders within your organization.

Your leadership comes from inside you. As you develop more leadership skills, you will become more confident in guiding your team's performance by modeling the behaviors you want to see. Research clearly supports the need for senior leadership's involvement in the leadership development process (Longenecker & Insch, 2018).

You will also learn from others in their mistakes and triumphs. We gently remind you to step back and seek to listen and understand before sharing your point of view. We talk about the art of reflection and the importance of constructive dialogue. We know that some situations will lead to places of discomfort, but your mindful approach to collaborative problem-solving and honest feedback can only strengthen the work that you are doing.

THE ISTE STANDARDS

This chapter speaks to ISTE **Education Leader Standard 3.5, Connected Learner**, wherein leaders model and promote continuous professional learning for themselves and others. We address guiding performance, providing avenues for accountability, reflecting, and identifying areas of growth for yourself. We are all continuous learners, and that's part of what makes you a Savvy Edtech Leader.

Create a Mission Propelled by *Why* and *How*

What value is a vision if a compelling purpose does not inspire it, and people need help understanding *why* and *how*? An inspiring purpose helps folks understand why your organization exists. The organization's purpose must answer the question *How does my organization position itself for success?* Edtech Leaders succeed when they figure out how to galvanize their team to buy into the purpose and understand the value of their contributions.

The vision reflects your organization's desired future. The purpose focuses on the present and why your team exists. The mission is embodied in the purpose statement because both are about what the organization does and who they do it for. An inspiring purpose helps bring the organization's vision to life.

 ## KEY STRATEGIES

- Create imagery to evoke a mental image of your purpose. Visual symbolism can help stir up emotions, so find images that inspire, energize, excite, and motivate you. Overlay your vision and purpose on top of your imagery.

- Reflect on your values regularly. Your core values are the principles that shape your decisions. Contemplate what matters most, what you stand for, and what you want to contribute to the organization.

- Use specific, measurable, achievable, relevant, and time-bound (SMART) goals that align with your purpose. Every goal must be meaningful and reflect what you want to achieve.

- Include your purpose statement in your communications. Keep the purpose alive and fresh in the organization's mind.

- Thread the purpose into conversations and discussions. Ask team members why they are working on specific tasks. Ask how they feel about their impact and contributions. Ask what they think their overarching purpose is. Ask what inspired them to take action. Remind everyone in the organization what the vision and purpose are every chance you get.

Suppose you have defined your organization's vision thus: *Where technology is always on, always fast, always innovative, and always seamless.* This vision may not represent the current situation. Your vision includes what you plan to be.

Circumstances may delay progress toward your vision. For example, you may need adequate funding or other resources to achieve your vision. You may be waiting on next year's budget, government funding, a grant, or a technology bond. An inspiring purpose will help you work towards creating the best possible technology experience now while planning to implement the systems and practices that lead to achieving the organization's vision.

An inspiring purpose statement could be: "Provide education technology systems and practices that maximize the technology experience and ensure student and educator success." The first part of the purpose statement, "Provide education technology systems and practices that maximize the technology experience," is what your organization does. The second part of the purpose statement, "ensure student and educator success," is the *why*.

The following guidelines show you how to develop an inspiring purpose.

Bring the team together to discuss the organization's purpose. The purpose is what the organization can do to move toward the vision with existing resources. The team should be familiar with the organization's existing capabilities. The team can identify synergies to define and inspire the purpose.

Brainstorm ideas with the team. Ask members of the team the following questions: *What is the focus of our organization? Why is what we do as a team necessary? What is each team member's unique value and contribution? What services do we provide? What are our current abilities and limitations? What are we trying to accomplish on behalf of our students and customers? What should our work be about? What do we do to inspire employee commitment? Does what we do define who we are and hope to be? What do we want to be known and remembered for?*

Craft a purpose statement. Add a compelling word or phrase that stirs emotions. For example, the expression world-class is captivating. Prepare to go through several iterations of the purpose statement until you are satisfied it reflects why your organization exists. Here are some examples of purpose statements aligning with the associated vision.

> VISION: Be the most innovative technology provider of K–12 digital solutions nationwide.
>
> PURPOSE: Deliver the best technologies to prepare students to be leaders in a global digital age.

> VISION: Trusted partners elevating education through innovative technology.
>
> PURPOSE: Educate students by providing innovative learning opportunities to develop technical knowledge and skills to empower them to be successful.

> VISION: The team that never wastes a second due to technology disruption.
>
> PURPOSE: Being proactive and intelligent so no one on our watch experiences technology disruption and thus has all the technology they need at their fingertips.

> VISION: Transformers of learning enabled by innovative technologies.
>
> PURPOSE: Transform lives by providing trusted service and all-the-time learning.

Remember, it's your organization's purpose. There's no right or wrong statement. It is crucial to help your team understand why their contributions impact the organization's success. An inspiring purpose guides your organization and sets you apart.

Create Harmony and Accountability

Guiding the performance of others is tricky, because we cannot reliably direct the behavior of those we lead. What we can do is guide their performance and steer them in the right direction. Thriving Edtech Leaders help team members reach the organization's goals and align with the organization's values, recognizing the significance of each team member's contributions.

Leaders must control our reaction to every staff member's behavior, from high performing to those who need improvement. Our responsibility is to deliver results and create harmony and accountability within the organization.

Harmony within the organization is based on congruent ideas, feelings, and actions that are consistent and in agreement with the team. Accountability promotes personal ownership. When staff members understand their work matters and their results are accountable to others, they will be more inclined to be committed and engaged.

Some staff members would prefer to work on their own schedule using their own prioritization system. When this happens, our leadership guidance is needed most. Why? Because those who depend on this sort of staff member will experience delays and be frustrated by the lack of consistency and transparency. Trust will be reduced. We can react by reassigning or doing the work ourselves, or we can effectively guide the staff member's performance.

 KEY STRATEGIES

- Keep your ears and eyes open. Walk around. If working remotely, check in virtually. Start informal conversations. Ask commonsense questions about the status of the organization's objectives.

- Act upon any hunch. Usually, our intuition is correct. Ask others their opinions about any performance issues that might be occurring.

- Don't let a problem fester. If you hear or see something, do something about it. We may think the concern will take care of itself. Sadly, it rarely does.

- Document, document, document. As time-consuming as it might be, accurate documentation is required.

- There is no room for a weak link on the team. Driving performance at the individual level rolls up to the organizational level, where harmony and accountability promote empowerment and ownership.

Create a Culture of Accountability

Every staff member is unique, but our leadership must be consistent. Motivations and development needs will vary, but our leadership must provide predictable, continuous feedback daily. When we are the leader, all eyes are on us. We must walk the walk, take ownership, and tailor our guidance and support to each individual, considering their strengths, aspirations, and circumstances.

The best Edtech Leaders maximize staff members' performance and foster long-term growth. Our leadership credibility is always on the line. Our reputation depends on getting results.

Set clear expectations. We must clearly define the performance expectations for each staff member, including specific goals, targets, and metrics aligned with organizational objectives. Staff members must understand expectations and how evaluation processes work. We must model back what we expect of others.

Give direct, immediate feedback. Recognize great work. When things need improvement, offer constructive feedback, focusing on exactly what needs improvement, with actionable suggestions.

Conduct performance reviews. Conduct formal performance reviews at regular intervals (e.g., annually or semiannually) to comprehensively assess staff members' performance. Use this opportunity to discuss their strengths, areas for improvement, and career development goals. Create a collaborative atmosphere where staff members feel comfortable sharing their perspectives and aspirations.

Offer coaching and mentoring. Offer one-on-one coaching sessions to discuss each team member's professional development, identify areas where they need support, and provide guidance on improving their performance.

Encourage ongoing learning and development. Support growth by providing access to training programs, workshops, seminars, or online courses. Encourage each staff member to acquire new skills, expand their knowledge, and stay updated with industry trends. Offer opportunities for job rotations or special projects to help them gain diverse experiences.

Establish clear communication channels. Maintain open lines of communication. Encourage staff members to share their ideas, concerns, and suggestions. Regularly communicate organizational updates, changes, and performance expectations to ensure everyone is on the same page.

Recognize and reward performance. Acknowledge and reward exceptional performance to motivate employees and reinforce positive behavior. Recognition can take various forms, such as verbal praise, written appreciation, financial incentives, promotions, or opportunities for advancement. Asking each employee how they like to be recognized will ensure they are recognized in a way in which they are comfortable.

Address performance issues immediately. If an employee's performance consistently falls below expectations, address the issue promptly. Identify the root causes of the problem and work collaboratively with the employee to develop a performance improvement plan. Offer additional support, training, or resources as needed.

The Gap between the Vision and the Work

As we work with individual staff members, there will always be gaps between the vision and the actual work required to drive high performance. How we address the gap between what *is* happening and what *must* be happening, then guiding performance to get back on track, is at the crux of our leadership success. We must ask tough questions and have difficult conversations when needed. We must hold every staff member accountable, including ourselves. We are responsible for recognizing and closing this gap before it becomes a gaping hole. Following are five escalating levels of guidance.

1. **You notice a slight crack.** Sometimes, it takes a quick mention, where we check in and ask questions lightheartedly. For example, "I noticed you have been late for work this week. Is everything okay?" Or, "I saw you didn't update your status on your completion report. Are there any issues that I might be able to help you with?"

2. **You see a widening gap.** Find an opportunity to address the issue in an informal, private conversation. For example, "Can we have a conversation

about your attendance? I'm noticing a pattern developing, and I'm concerned about you and want to help."

3. **The gap widens and leads to crumbling.** Schedule a formal meeting where you emphasize the importance and urgency around the problem, and where the focus is on the resolution. Focus on concrete behaviors with specific examples. For example, "You have missed a key milestone, and now our team is behind schedule. We must discuss a specific action plan to get back on track. I look forward to hearing what you think needs to be done." Record the details and formally send the document to the staff member. Here's the key, and it sounds easy, but many leaders do not do this one thing: document the conversation and follow up with the staff member about a specific action plan. Once the documentation begins, talk with the human resources department and let them know a staff member is working toward a plan of improvement.

4. **The gap is huge, and the staff member is falling into it.** You must set boundaries around the concern and find a way to lift this staffer up and out of the gap. Schedule a formal meeting and invite a human resources representative to join you. Emphasize the severity of the issue. Let them know the specific consequences if performance is not improved. Prior documentation works to your advantage in these situations, because you are building a case for disciplinary action.

5. **The staff member hits rock bottom.** Performance is at an all-time low. Your guidance may include the following: A formal performance improvement plan with a specific action plan or a recommendation to human resources for disciplinary action. Prepare the documentation in advance. Deliver the documentation to the employee in a formal meeting. Remember that some environments may require you to have a human resources representative present at the meeting. At the meeting's conclusion, you and the staffer should sign the documentation. If they will not sign, document their failure to comply with your request.

Savvy Edtech Leaders can guide performance in many ways, including acknowledging the gaps, creating measurable expectations within a time-bound period, and providing frequent feedback. How we guide performance with compelling dialogue and documentation separates good leaders from extraordinary leaders.

Model the Standard for Success

Horace Mann, the father of American education, wrote, "They who set an example make a highway. Others follow the example because it is easier to travel on a highway than over untrodden grounds." Humans often copy traits and skills from each other. This ability is described as "modeling."

Modeling, also known as social learning or observational learning, occurs when an individual observes and imitates the behavior of another person. It involves acquiring new behaviors, skills, attitudes, and values by observing and replicating the actions of others.

The modeling process can be intentional or unintentional, involving positive and negative behaviors. We must be thoughtful and deliberate as we contemplate modeling others. Resolve to be mindful and actively promote positive modeling behaviors. The importance of self-reflection and self-awareness when modeling others cannot be overstated. Ask yourself why you are drawn to certain qualities and behaviors in others, and make sure you choose to model behaviors that align with your own values and goals.

 ## KEY STRATEGIES

- Recognize people whom you deem successful, study their habits and behaviors, and understand the factors that contributed to their success. Begin to incorporate their positive traits into your own behavior.

- Establish goals that align with your aspirations, and track your progress towards them. Celebrate your accomplishments, big or small, to maintain motivation and momentum throughout your personal journey of self-improvement.

- Prioritize continuous learning and adaptability. Embrace a mindset of lifelong learning and stay updated with new developments in your field. Understand that failure is a natural part of growth, and see challenges as opportunities for improvement and learning.

- Cultivate a strong support network. Surround yourself with supportive and encouraging individuals. Share your experiences and insights with others to positively impact their lives and contribute to their growth.

- Promote accountability and embody the modeled behaviors. Take ownership of your actions, learn from your mistakes, and take responsibility for successes and failures.

Modeling can be a significant factor in the development of human behavior, as it allows individuals to learn new behaviors quickly and effectively by observing and imitating others. Through modeling, individuals can acquire social skills, communication strategies, and problem-solving techniques. This strategy can benefit Edtech Leaders as we seek to grow, improve our performance, and positively influence others.

As you identify the qualities and behaviors that successful people exhibit and then adopt those traits and behaviors in your own life, there are some strategies that you can use to model success. Following are some steps to model success and adapt the behaviors of successful individuals.

First, identify people whom you consider successful. This can include individuals in your industry, celebrities, or even friends and family who have achieved their goals. Once you have identified these successful individuals, study their habits and behaviors. Observe their work ethic, time management skills, communication style, and other inspirational traits.

Analyze the factors that contributed to their success. Consider their education, experience, connections, and personal qualities. By understanding these aspects, you can gain insights into the paths they took and the strategies they employed to achieve success.

Once you have identified relevant habits and behaviors of successful people, it's time to start emulating them in your own life. Incorporate their positive habits into your daily routine. For example, if successful individuals prioritize their health and fitness, consider integrating regular exercise and healthy eating habits into your lifestyle. Additionally, if you are friends with your role model, share with them what behaviors you are trying to emulate. Chances are they will be flattered by your inquiry and would be honored to share some of their secrets to success!

It's important to stay motivated throughout the process of modeling success. Set goals for yourself that align with your aspirations, and track your progress. Celebrate your accomplishments, no matter how small, to maintain motivation and momentum.

As an Edtech Leader (or aspiring Edtech Leader), find opportunities to model success for others. Modeling success for others involves demonstrating positive behavior, habits, and mindsets that can help them achieve their goals, focusing on behaviors and actions that have led to success in a particular area. Following are steps you can take to model success for others.

To get started, reflect on what you did to succeed in a particular area. Identify the specific behaviors, activities, and strategies that were most effective for you.

If part of your success involved creating specific, measurable, achievable, relevant, and time-bound (SMART) goals, share them with others to inspire them to develop their goals.

Adopting and embracing a growth mindset and believing you can improve and learn from your experiences is a tactic you can model so others learn to see challenges as opportunities for growth. Failure is a natural part of the process. Failure provides valuable feedback that can help anyone improve their approach. Instead of giving up, we should use failure as an opportunity to learn and grow.

You can model a strong work ethic by showing dedication, persistence, and resilience in pursuing your goals. In prioritizing tasks, setting deadlines, and staying organized, you provide a model of efficiency that will inspire others to follow you.

Continuous learning and adaptability are key factors for success. It is important to nurture a sense of curiosity and stay updated with new developments in your field. Surrounding yourself with supportive and encouraging individuals is crucial. Seek guidance and advice from mentors or coaches who have already achieved the success you aspire to reach. Their wisdom and experience can provide invaluable insights and help navigate challenges.

Share your experiences and insights as a powerful way to inspire and guide others. Identify the behaviors and actions that have contributed to your success, and impart this knowledge through mentoring, coaching, or creating content such as blogs, podcasts, or videos.

Effective communication skills are essential in all aspects of life. Developing strong communication skills, actively listening, and expressing opinions fosters understanding and collaboration. Encourage open communication and feedback in your relationships, fostering a supportive and constructive environment.

Prioritizing self-care is fundamental to success. Maintaining physical, mental, and emotional well-being through healthy eating, regular exercise, sufficient sleep, and stress management is vital. By practicing self-care, you become more resilient and better equipped to handle the demands of life. Encourage others to prioritize their well-being as well.

Providing feedback and support to others is crucial in their pursuit of success. As they seek to model their actions based on your example, offer guidance and constructive feedback. Encourage them to explore new strategies, and be there to provide support when needed. You can create a collaborative and empowering environment that promotes growth and achievement.

You can best model success for others by defining your precise goals, taking consistent and focused action towards those goals, learning from failure, seeking support and guidance, and celebrating achievements. By following these steps and maintaining a positive mindset, individuals can set a strong example of success and inspire others to do the same.

Learn from Everyone in the Room

In a world filled with diverse opinions, learning from others should be an enriching experience that broadens our perspectives and fosters personal growth. Edtech Leaders often quote David Weinberger, who wrote, "The smartest person in the room is the room itself (2014)." What happens when there are points of view in the room with which we disagree?

This section will guide us through embracing differing viewpoints, finding common ground, and cultivating empathy while maintaining a respectful and open-minded approach. Discover the value of engaging in constructive dialogue, challenging your beliefs, and appreciating the learning opportunities that disagreements present.

 KEY STRATEGIES

- Maintain an open mind and seek understanding. Any time you find yourself in a group of people, focus your attention on the person speaking and genuinely take an interest in what they have to say.

- Engage in constructive dialogue and maintain respectful communication. Whenever you are in a group of people exchanging ideas, always strive to promote a civil and inclusive atmosphere for discussion.

- Embrace challenging assumptions and consider alternative perspectives. Be open to modifying your original thinking.

- Reflect on all points of view. Respect and appreciate the experiences of others that shaped their point of view.

Maintain an Open Mind

Listen attentively, without interrupting, to fully understand the speaker's viewpoint. We often prepare our statements or, when we disagree, our rebuttal in our heads while someone speaks, and we miss major points. Consider ways you might modify their ideas to make them more applicable to your situation instead of disregarding them completely.

When the person speaking takes a breath or finishes their thought, glance around the group and take note of the body language of others to get a temperature reading on how the conversation is affecting the group. You might need to diffuse a situation, or you may need to be more diplomatic than usual with your response. To maintain an open mind and continue an open dialogue, set aside your biases and judgments and embrace the diversity of perspectives, recognizing that differing viewpoints offer valuable insights. Be receptive to new ideas and possibilities, even if they contradict your beliefs, and resist the urge to immediately dismiss or disregard opinions that differ from yours. Dig deeper to uncover the underlying reasons and motivations behind others' opinions and ask probing questions encouraging a deeper exploration of their perspective. Make a genuine effort to understand their experiences and the context that shaped their viewpoint.

Engage in Constructive Dialogue

To foster an environment of mutual respect, avoid personal attacks, laying blame, and dismissive behavior. When the timing is right during the exchange of ideas, be curious and ask follow-up questions to delve deeper into the opposing viewpoints. Aim for meaningful conversations that promote understanding rather than winning the debate. Express your disagreement with respect and courtesy, focusing on the merits of the ideas.

To have productive conversations with differing viewpoints, find some common ground. Look for shared goals or values that can serve as a basis for agreement or compromise. Identify areas of overlap where collaboration and understanding can be encouraged, emphasizing the importance of building bridges and finding commonalities that transcend differing opinions. We can promote inclusivity and mutual respect. Utilizing neutral language is key; before expressing disagreement, it's crucial to acknowledge the thoughts and expertise of others, highlighting the strong points in their ideas. This approach demonstrates active listening and ensures clarity, mitigating the risk of misunderstanding. Functional phrases such as "in my experience," "my concerns are," or "in my opinion" should precede contra-dicting viewpoints, fostering an environment conducive to meaningful discourse and consensus-building.

Consider Alternative Perspectives

Recognize that engaging with different viewpoints can expand your understanding and modify your thinking. We can learn from every workshop or meeting we attend. Even if you learn what you don't agree with, that is learning. When ques-tioning why you disagree, you must also question your own thinking or actions.

Savvy Edtech Leaders use these conversations to challenge their assumptions and beliefs and are open to altering their perspectives. Approach disagreements as opportunities for personal growth and intellectual development. After a conver-sation, take time to reflect on points of disagreement and evaluate their potential validity.

Reflect and Appreciate

We do not encourage hostile disagreements or disagreeing for the sake of debate, but we do encourage you to surround yourself with people with different strengths and viewpoints. Surrounding yourself only with like-minded people who always agree with you will keep you from growing and evolving. As you reflect on conver-sations where you have disagreed with a speaker, have empathy, be curious, and appreciate the value of diverse perspectives in expanding your knowledge and understanding. To develop empathy, consider the following:

- Put yourself in others' shoes, considering their unique experiences and backgrounds.

- Understand the context that shaped their viewpoint.

- Approach disagreements with compassion, seeking to understand rather than judge.

Recognize that respectful and constructive debates offer intellectual growth and the chance to refine your ideas and broaden your horizons. Cultivate a culture of open dialogue where differing opinions are welcomed and valued. Even when you disagree, learning from others has value. By practicing active listening, maintaining an open mind, and engaging in constructive dialogue, you can bridge divides, find common ground, and appreciate the learning opportunities presented by disagreements. Embrace this journey of empathy and growth, increasing connections and expanding your horizons.

Be the Best of the Best

Ultimately, only one person is responsible for your growth and development: you. You might have a manager or mentor who pushes you, but it's up to you to lead your journey. No one cares more than you do!

Acknowledging where you are now in your profession is a reality check. Do you have the career or job title you thought you would have by now? If not, why? Do you blame your perceived failure on factors out of your control, like ethnicity, gender, or organizational politics? If so, stop. Focus your energy on committing to being the best of the best. Then, there's no question. Over time, others will see it. And if they don't, it's their loss, not yours!

 KEY STRATEGIES

- Surround yourself with the best people. Your colleagues will shape you more than anything else. Spend time with talented, inspired, growing people.

- Get educated and certified. Get that degree, that next-level certification, and another on top of that one. Get that association affiliation title!

- Access the best speakers and learning providers. Listen to podcasts rather than the radio. Spend time learning about future trends.

- Attend great events. Go to conferences that help you grow and get inspired. Planning your next big event should always be on your mind.

- Read leadership improvement books. Think of each book as connecting with a mentor. Mentors who help you improve to be your best are more valuable than you can imagine.

Escape the Victim Mentality

The victim mentality in a professional context is when we feel overlooked for a promotion or job opportunity because of external circumstances beyond our control. A typical victim mentality response might be, "No matter what I do, no one seems to notice" or "I just need one person to give me a break, then I can prove I can do the job." Another example is, "Others get promoted before me because of who they know." Why do we do this? Because it's easier to play the victim and expect others to change so we don't have to. Ouch!

How do we fix this? We can escape the victim mentality by acknowledging our current professional level and accepting it as entirely justified and something to learn from. Once we accept our current state, we stop whining, moaning, and groaning to others about why we can't get a break. We stop wallowing in our injustices. We forget about blaming others for our current circumstances. Taking full responsibility for ourselves is liberating.

Where Do You Need to Grow?

One big key to successful personal development is to grow in your areas of strength. Why is this so powerful? Because if you can master the areas where you are strongest, you'll find yourself head and shoulders above the crowd. If you get bogged down in your weaker areas, you might waste valuable energy on a skill and never rise above average. Target your strengths.

> **TOASTMASTERS TO THE RESCUE**
>
> For many years in my career, I felt insecure about communicating in front of influential leaders. I was a great communicator amongst my peers and staff. But when I got up in front of the superintendent or the board of trustees, often I would freeze. Was I insecure? Maybe. Did I need better communication skills? Not really. Did I care too much about how those at a higher level perceived me? Yes! What did I do to learn how to overcome my fear? I joined Toastmasters. Others recognized my improvement. I told them about my growth plan. Then they expressed an interest in joining, so I set up a Toastmasters chapter for my organization, and then everyone on my team started learning and improving!
>
> — FRANKIE JACKSON

Learn, Baby, Learn

What is your professional learning growth plan? If you don't have a plan, start developing one today. Learning is not an automatic process. You must schedule time for it. You may have heard the adage "What gets scheduled gets done." Your plan must be designed to meet your career aspirations. Following are some basic learning plan principles that may help.

Your plan doesn't need to be elaborate—it just needs to be specific, so you will commit to it and get it done. Include learning new skills that will help set you apart from everyone else. Those who commit to learning and being the best in their craft are noticed.

Capitalize on your greatest strengths. Whatever you are best at, wherever your strongest skill is, and that thing that makes you come alive: that's your superpower! Continue learning new skills that ignite the best in you. Save time by not getting bogged down in your weaker areas.

Lighting the Path Forward
How Energy and Enthusiasm Fuel Empowerment

How can we be enthusiastic, energetic, and lively when striving to be an empowering leader? How do we inspire others to change their behavior based on our leadership strategy? It's complex. Empowering and leading people requires an excessive amount of energy and enthusiasm. We must set the direction. We must align the work and move our organization forward to achieve goals and objectives. We must inspire others to complete projects and provide service. As leaders, we must motivate others to achieve high performance and empower them to collaborate, from beginning to end, with the same level of enthusiasm. Who has a recipe for that?

Acclaimed author and speaker Jon Gordon reminds us to choose enthusiasm and optimism as our guiding light instead of being defined by circumstances and events (Gordon, 2021). One way is to use our internal compass, our light from within, to help create more alignment, because energy bubbles up from the inside out. Our energy shapes our values and sparks enthusiasm for us to change. We may then lead with greater purpose, shaping our values and empowering others with a readiness to change.

The ISTE **Empowering Leader Standard 3.3** underpins this chapter, lighting the path forward with energy and enthusiasm. The Savvy Edtech Leader builds their leadership craft with interpersonal skills that combine social skills, communication skills, personality qualities, attitudes, and emotional intelligence. This unique blend of skills, fueled with energy and enthusiasm, fosters an innovative, inclusive culture with a sense of belonging, where everyone's perspectives are valued and respected. Isn't that how empowering leaders build professional agency and leadership skills in others, where individuals feel empowered, motivated, and inspired to reach their full potential? Savvy Edtech Leaders focus on creating empowered leaders who light the path forward for others.

Embrace Oozy, Woozy Enthusiasm

Many factors contribute to thriving Edtech Leadership, but one that is often overlooked and undervalued is enthusiasm. We're talking about the level of enthusiasm that oozes positive energy. It is an inner spark that keeps us moving forward with optimism and hope, day after day, moment by moment. The word enthusiasm is rooted in the Greek word *enthousiasmos* and means inspired by a higher power. Without it, we fizzle out.

 ## KEY STRATEGIES

- Create more fun at work. A little bit of fun can be a breath of fresh air for everyone, especially when work is stressful.

- Recognize enthusiasm in others. It's simple to say, "You made my day a little bit brighter by lifting my spirits; thank you!"

- Celebrate every project milestone and personal event. Who doesn't like to celebrate? It could be ice cream bars or a waffle breakfast. Do whatever it takes to get team members to smile and be happy.

- Get out, walk around, or meet with your team online for lunch. Breaking bread together has always led to bonding. Why not do that with your team?

- Encourage heartfelt, enthusiastic conversations. Why not start any meeting or conversation with the question: "What are you enthusiastic about today?"

Enthusiastic Leaders Are Contagious

Some might ask, how can we feel eager when we must wake up, go to a stressful job, and work with unenthusiastic people? Or how can we feel enthusiastic when we have "xyz" to do today, or worse, no plan for the day? To be an enthusiastic leader, we must find ways to keep our inner flame burning, no matter what the day brings.

It's easy to exude enthusiasm when the day is going great. But what do we do when our fire begins to lose its spark? What will we do to rekindle our flame? The key is to find your oozy, woozy enthusiasm.

When we see others gushing with enthusiasm about something, it naturally makes us want to feel that same excitement. As leaders, when we exude enthusiasm, we influence others to stay motivated and energized about our organization's work. That's a powerful motivator! How do we get others to adopt the same spirit?

Connect Enthusiasm to Team's Vision, Purpose, and Goals

Perhaps your team is not as enthusiastic as you are about the organization's vision, mission, and goals. Following are some intentional things we can do to stimulate enthusiasm in others.

Find uninhibited times to talk with our team about how we translate the vision into a concept we can get excited about. For example, if a team member's job includes ensuring the internet is available 24/7, ask what that might mean to a student trying to learn or a teacher trying to develop lesson plans. Spawn conversations in

> ### MR. CHARISMA
>
> I was honored to work with Jack Grayson, CEO of the American Productivity & Quality Center, as my mentor. He was known as Mr. Charisma and inspired others with his acute listening skills and knack for knowing when to inject into the conversation. He would share a story, a book, or a quote that would contextualize any conversation with creativity. As a great mentor, he always lifted others. That's that kind of oozy, woozy enthusiasm that connects with others.
>
> — FRANKIE JACKSON

meetings about how the team's purpose connects to what motivates them in their current role. Ask about a goal a team member is working on that is exciting. Share enthusiastic stories about yourself and others excited about what they are doing. Find reasons to surround yourself with those types of people more.

Raise the Levels of Liveliness around You

Think about a time when you were around someone who walked into a room or joined a conversation, and you could feel their energy raising the levels of the liveliness in those around them. I bet you couldn't keep your eyes off them. I bet you listened to everything they said and felt inspired. I imagine others feel the same as you. When I see someone like that, I think, wow, whatever they've got, I want it!

What is it that they do? What is this energy they bring with them wherever they go? In an instant, they charm and influence everyone around them. How do they raise the energy levels in the room? How do they make everyone come alive just by their presence? What if we could bundle up that energy and affect others similarly?

 ## KEY STRATEGIES

- Conduct an energy audit. Notice what drains your energy. If possible, divert your attention away from things that drain your energy. Move on and reenergize yourself quickly.

- Be aware of when you procrastinate. Why? You may not be motivated by that particular task or person. Could you delegate or outsource it?

- Build at least one energizing activity into your day first thing. That might be exercising, meditating, or reading.

- Stop and recharge when you drop below 100%. Charge up with a lively friend or colleague. Do whatever it takes to charge yourself to lead at total capacity.

Aim for a 100% Charge

To be the charismatic, energetic leader, you must try to keep your energy levels near 100%. You must develop healthy sleep patterns, diet, physical activity, and stress management tactics. Following are some strategies to stay supercharged:

- Get sufficient sleep. Consistent and restorative sleep is crucial for replenishing energy levels and overall well-being.

- Follow a balanced diet. We know what a well-balanced diet is. It's up to us to be disciplined and stick to it.

- Stay hydrated. Dehydration can cause fatigue, so drink plenty of water throughout the day to maintain optimal energy levels.

- Prioritize regular exercise. Regular physical activity can boost your energy and improve overall stamina.

- Take breaks. Give yourself short breaks throughout the day to recharge. Stepping away from work can help you return with renewed focus.

- Manage stress. Chronic stress can drain your energy. Find healthy ways to manage stress, such as meditation, breathing exercises, or hobbies you enjoy.

- Create a consistent routine. Consistency can regulate your body's internal clock and improve energy levels.

- Avoid overworking. Know your limits and avoid overextending yourself. Prioritize tasks and delegate, when possible, to prevent burnout.

An Energy Exchange

What if there were a gadget to measure the flow of energy between people? In every interaction, we are increasing, decreasing, or maintaining our energy level. A fundamental question to ask ourselves is, when we show up, does everyone else's energy level go up? At minimum, Edtech Leaders should feed positive energy.

The best Edtech Leaders take it a step further. They develop a unique ability to attract others, just like a magnet, and gain their support. Have you ever worked with a leader where you thought, "I don't know where they are going, but wherever it is, count me in." That's a leader with high levels of energetic influence!

Be an Energy Magnet

Try these simple magnetizing energy strategies to energize yourself first, then magnetize that energy in those around you.

Just say *yes* enthusiastically. Anytime we say yes, and we say it with a smile, our energy level increases. Try it. Say yes out loud right now. Can you feel it? Others will feel it, too, and their energy will increase.

Surround yourself with others that energize you. Magnetism is powerful. People are attracted to others with similar characteristics, values, energy levels, abilities, and backgrounds. If the organization isn't performing, assess yourself first. We attract who we are, not who we want. If you have an area of weakness, recruit others that are different so you can combine energies.

Dig deep. If you want the organization to be more committed to those it serves, double-check yourself. Are you demonstrating a commitment to customers? Are you following up? Are you visiting those you serve? Are you adding value? Are you showing in conversations with your staff that you are committed to your customers? We must represent what we desire in others.

Create an energizing physical environment. A messy physical space may distract you more than you realize. Surround yourself with a pleasing aroma, inspiring images, a bright workspace, or whatever increases your energy.

Bring out the best in others. Use your energy to lift the energy of others. Find ways to inspire your team so they strive for excellence. The high-performing leader knows how to bring out the energies of those they lead.

Make magnetizing-energy activities your life's game plan. Be creative in delegating tasks that drain your energy.

Manage your energy, not your time. Start the day with the most exciting tasks first; it builds momentum. Batch up the energy-draining tasks so you can mix those tasks with exciting ones.

Your ability to shift the energy of those you lead is critical to your success. With energy, things get done. When our energy tank is at 100%, we are more motivated. Make sure your energy is at the level you desire in others. Then, be a magnet in attracting others to perform at the same high level.

Shape the Organization's Values

Values are not just words on a page; they are guiding principles that inspire and govern an organization's actions and decision making. They form the bedrock of the organization's culture and expected behaviors. To shape the organization's values, set clear expectations and recognize the behaviors that exemplify our values.

Savvy Edtech Leaders must be creative in reinforcing the organization's values and making our employees feel valued and integral to our services and support. How do we decide on a set of values for our team? Even more challenging is how we define and live by our organization's value declarations.

The National Institute of Standards and Technology's Baldrige Performance Excellence Program for Education Framework (2023–24) defines values as "the guiding principles and behaviors that embody how your organization and its people are expected to operate." Defining our values requires an intense study of our culture and vision. Consider how you will use your values to demonstrate what we hope to achieve and represent. When establishing your organization's values, consider these key strategies.

 ## KEY STRATEGIES

- Keep it real. Create values that are easy for your organization's employees to remember and embody. Distill your values down to the simple words that the average person understands. Consider the authentic meaning of your values.

- Be transparent. Creating values that are vague and filled with empty jargon dilutes your authenticity. Values need to align with your vision and goals. They should be relevant to the services and support your organization offers.

- Build distinctive values that are worth remembering. Values need to be intrinsic, embedded beliefs and behaviors that form the foundation of your organization. Consider what is unique about your leadership and your organization.

- Align your values based on the why. Think of your why as a filter used to make the most impactful decisions about what you truly value. When needed, realign your values based on your why, which may mean reprioritizing or letting one or more values go.

- Create a mental image of your values. Use descriptors to align your mental image to your why. Using a visual representation will help you visualize the culture and behaviors you are trying to build.

Let the Values Guide the Culture

Our values are not just words on a page; they are the compass that guides an organization's culture, influencing every employee and every decision we make. They are not just a set of rules; they are our North Star, ensuring that we always make the right choices. We need clear, meaningful values that everyone can buy into. Consider the success of a high-performing mega–school district, which captured the essence of its culture by putting its values into practice. This led the organization to sustained success, a testament to the power of well-implemented values. Below is an example of this organization's values with explicit behavior descriptors.

The organization developed six core values: efficient, accessible, systematic, student-focused, service-oriented, highly-skilled, and leadership. For each value, specific behaviors are described. With this level of detail, employees can share common values and act in ways that are congruent with the values, leading to the expansion of a shared culture. This shared culture is not just a concept; it's a bond that unites the organization, making the team stronger and more successful together.

Efficient. Sharing time, resources, and information; involving others; being open-minded; continuing to challenge the status quo; modifying plans in response to changing conditions; being action-oriented and results-driven; tackling problems head-on; accomplishing daily work tasks; working independently; defining processes that lead to efficiency.

Accessible. Acknowledging all customer and employee communication within 24 hours; balancing competing priorities; listening, paying attention, and understanding customer requests; being approachable and welcoming questions; gaining trust by being available; recognizing the importance of following proper chain of command.

Systematic. Using critical indicators and management systems to monitor results; documenting key processes; standardizing to provide reliable offerings; aligning strategic objectives, action plans, and work systems; managing the whole organization with a systems perspective; analyzing data to determine trends, projections, and cause and effect; thinking out of the box.

Student-focused. Keeping pace with rapid changes in technology to support 21st-century skills and learning; developing technology solutions with the capacity to provide faster and more flexible emerging technologies for students;

keeping students safe and secure, including their identities; sustaining technology services that are available one hundred percent of the time for students; communicating information about technology.

Service-oriented. Developing long-term relationships; seeking input from customers; being flexible and patient; exercising good listening skills when providing service to customers; establishing clear-cut agreements, setting realistic expectations, and following up with customers; aligning technology and support; maintaining a big-picture perspective.

Highly skilled. Mastering new technical knowledge and skills; anticipating risks and devising contingency plans; involving teams of others with the skills and expertise to contribute; keeping skills current; taking responsibility for actions; seeking greater roles and responsibilities; integrating innovation; handling pressure well.

Leadership. Communicating directly, honestly, and respectfully; communicating in all forms of speaking, writing, and presenting, using emerging technologies and aligning the message to the customer; being innovative by bringing meaningful change that leads to improving services and increasing value; exhibiting courage by having difficult conversations and pulling back when technology solutions do not address a real need; being results-oriented, focusing on measurement of results and continuous improvement; staying one step ahead in organizing staff to meet the increasing demands of the organization.

As you read these values with specific descriptors, think about your organization. What type of behavior will increase its energy and enthusiasm? Will these behaviors create feelings of empowerment to embody these values in their work and interactions?

EMPLOYEE RECOGNITION

Frankie Jackson says that recognizing employees who embody the organization's values connects the team and increases engagement. She based recognition programs on employees who best demonstrated the organization's values for a given month or year. This form of recognition connected the team and the culture. She also saw an increase in customer satisfaction and team spirit. Employee recognition is one of the best ways to enhance employee morale as it validates efforts, increases motivation, and contributes to a positive and supportive work environment.

Tips to Develop a Set of Values

Following are some additional tips that can help you jump-start the process of shaping your organization's values.

- Define the values that, as a Savvy Edtech Leader, you know are important to the organization. Go through the complete process of defining the values in advance. It is our primary responsibility to build a high-performing organization. Start with the core values that align with your vision and beliefs.

- Once you have developed the basis for the organization's core values, it is time to get input and buy-in from the organization. Brainstorm core values with our key team leaders and employees.

- Make a values discussion part of regular meetings. Carve out time on the agenda to discuss core values from the perspective of what is vital to the organization. This collaborative effort will result in a more comprehensive understanding of the values and ensure buy-in from the organization.

  - Start the core values discussion by starting with the organization's vision, purpose, and beliefs. Ask easy questions such as: *What essential qualities must every employee possess? What behaviors and attitudes do we want all employees to adhere to regardless of their position? How do we treat others? What do we admire most about the employees in our organization? What behaviors best exemplify the organization's culture?*

  - List the qualities and look for patterns. Start with your list of core values as a catalyst for discussion. Use the information you gather to improve the final version of your organization's core values. Ensure everyone agrees to the definitive list of qualities that make up the core values. The aim is to build a list of core values everyone commits to.

- Identify categories. Build models of similar characteristics. Think about the traits your group wants to demonstrate. For example, a value category may be talented if one of your beliefs is to provide innovative technology to enable the success of our students, educators, educational leaders, and coaches. If another belief is that innovative technology can change the trajectory of our students and positively impact learning, then a category might be student-focused. Look for five or six broad categories. Too many categories should be whittled down.

- Define each value category and make each value category distinct. Describe what the value category means by identifying the characteristics that make your organization unique. Finalize the categories and make them memorable. As you finalize the categories, consider how your organization will communicate the values. You want to make them resonate with everyone. If you can shape the value categories into a memorable and meaningful acronym, they will be easier to remember. Here is an example of five value categories that spell TRUST when creatively assembled.

    Talented. Advanced technical, academic, and interpersonal skills with the capacity to lead, solve problems, serve, innovate, and grow.

    Reliable. Consistent performance by being dependable and trustworthy in all interactions.

    Ubiquitous. Widespread ability to connect and use technology everywhere and anytime seamlessly and safely.

    Student-focused. Provide innovative learning opportunities for students that extend their abilities through rich, collaborative, engaging educational experiences.

    Transparent. Serve authentically, free from pretense, and always in a clear, honest, trustworthy manner.

- Communicate the organization's values. Creative communication is where the fun begins. Once you have finalized the values, share them! Weave them into your website and social media. Create posters, shirts, coffee mugs, or business cards to build momentum. In conversations and presentations with customers and staff, tell stories that emphasize the demonstrated values. Find quotes that correlate with the values. Be creative in how you consistently communicate what the values mean to you.

- Reinforce the values. Keep the values at the forefront of your leadership. Display them in your office, website, social media, and publications. Hire prospective employees based on their values. Promote and reward employees based on the demonstration of set performance expectations. Performance expectations direct everyone in the organization to express commitment to the culture you are working to create. Leaders evaluate staff by describing how they expect them to demonstrate the organization's values. Values are your culture's personality, so be proud and promote them.

- Set performance expectations for everyone you lead. Performance expectations direct everyone in the organization to express commitment to the culture. Leaders evaluate staff by describing how they expect them to demonstrate the organization's values.

- Notice what is important to you. What is important is what we want to import into our lives. Whatever your highest values are, when we live according to them, we can't wait to get up in the morning and share what is inside our hearts and souls with the organization. The organization can't wait to receive our service. The organization on the outside will reflect the organization on the inside.

- Use your imagination to push your vision. The organization's vitality is directly proportionate to the vividness of our vision. The clarity of our message is the power of our calling. When we are empowered and purposeful, we are successful leaders.

- Serve the people in your organization. When we dedicate our lives to serving others, we do valuable things. Our values shine through in everything we do. People pay us because we value ourselves. When we love what we do and do what we love, our mental and physical bodies support us in doing extraordinary things.

Empower Others

A piece of leadership advice attributed to Bill Gates is "As we look ahead into the next century, leaders will be those who empower others." Real leaders nurture future leaders during their lifetime, recognizing that leadership is essentially a baton that must be passed on. You may have positively influenced many individuals, though they might not express it. Even if you haven't personally met them, your actions may have made their lives better. Often, leadership is misconceived as exerting authority and displaying superior knowledge or qualifications compared to others. However, the true essence of leadership involves fostering an environment where others can surpass their perceived limitations.

Edith Wharton wrote that the spreading of enlightenment can occur in two manners: by being the source of light, like a candle, or by being a mirror that reflects light onto others (Wharton, 1902). Legitimate strength comes from empowering others. Enabling others doesn't reduce your own power but *magnifies* it. Authentic leadership focuses on bolstering its followers. It involves educating, leading by example, and empowering others. If you aspire to lead, your effectiveness will be gauged by the accomplishments of those around you.

Empowerment aims to equip your team members with the necessary knowledge and autonomy to tackle issues and meet organizational objectives. When individuals have the tools to solve problems, it liberates their time to explore and grow in other aspects. Numerous methods exist to foster empowerment in the workplace.

 ## KEY STRATEGIES

- Foster collaboration and autonomy. Encourage active engagement, value input, and trust your team to use their skills and knowledge independently. Emphasize teamwork and avoid micromanagement. This balance increases efficiency.

- Maintain positivity and gratitude. Convey an optimistic attitude during challenges and express gratitude consistently. A positive environment fosters team members' enthusiasm, and appreciation encourages continued efforts and builds trust.

- Understand and support team goals. Get to know the individual career aspirations of your team members. Offer your support, providing opportunities for them to learn new skills or discover hidden strengths. This approach encourages them to retain a sense of control and choice in their career path.

- Lead by example. Demonstrate the behaviors and work ethics you want your team to adopt. This approach is far more effective than dictating behaviors and fosters a more respectful and productive environment.

- Offer support when team members struggle and acknowledge their successes. Helping team members surmount challenges and publicly recognizing their achievements empowers and motivates them to strive for consistently high performance.

Empowerment through Trust

Sometimes, we must trust others to take charge of particular tasks or goals without extensive supervision. Although delegating such responsibility, especially when you may bear the brunt of their errors, might be discomforting, it is essential for fostering empowerment. Everyone makes mistakes. Allow people to learn from their errors and move on without losing your trust. If you're in a leadership role, it's important to show understanding when teammates err, particularly in the initial stages. Communicate to your team members that it's natural and anticipated that some mistakes will happen.

Seeking feedback is another critical component of empowering others. This is especially important for Edtech Leaders, managers, or supervisors. One of the most effective strategies for empowering others is just asking what they require. Whether their sense of empowerment is undermined due to micromanagement or lack of access to certain information, initiating these discussions can enhance empowerment for everyone.

Confidence Building and Acknowledgement

You can quickly empower others to gain confidence in their performance by providing guidance. When an employee uniquely knows how to accomplish a task that others don't, they often spend significant time addressing others' issues. In such cases, it's helpful to align everyone by giving clear instructions or conducting training sessions. Disseminate understanding among team members to foster a self-reliant, empowering work environment. Developing instructional and informational materials is a significant move towards empowering your team, but it only proves effective if team members can quickly discover and utilize the information. The most efficient way to instruct others on completing their tasks is to share the guidelines in an easily accessible shared space. Investing time to provide a straightforward, direct method for accessing information and learning autonomously boosts productivity. Individuals needing specific information can find it, and current "experts" aren't perpetually teaching others.

One of the most potent means to empower others is to acknowledge their hard work. Giving positive feedback and expressing gratitude for demonstrating responsibility and initiative encourages proactive behavior and instills a sense of worth, thus promoting a positive work environment. This sense of empowerment is contagious. As employees see that efforts and positive results are recognized and celebrated, they are more apt to step up and work to receive recognition.

Signature Edtech Leadership
*Crafting an Authentic, Influential,
and Innovative Approach*

As a Savvy Edtech Leader, you likely already realize that navigating the dynamic world of K–12 education today requires a multifaceted approach. Begin by crafting a road map that guides through and reflects on both successes and failures. Dive into the data, observe, actively listen, and communicate with intention. Embrace innovative thinking and glean insights from every experience, whether positive or negative. Savvy Edtech Leaders scrutinize the outcomes of previous choices and explore multiple pathways to successful resolutions.

Effective Edtech Leaders aren't just managers and leaders; they are talent discoverers. Armed with courage, they unearth hidden potential in others (Brown, 2018). Striking a balance between authority and empowerment, they invest time in forging authentic connections, understanding their team, and nurturing mutual commitment and trust. Research has found that organizations need leaders who are accomplished at motivating employees so that the employees can demonstrate positive behaviors to maintain stability and benefit the organization, especially when those behaviors are not officially stated as part of the job description (Yamak and Eyupoglu, 2021).

As you synthesize the insights and strategies in this chapter, establish clear goals and actionable steps to set the stage for progress. Continuous evaluation and adjustment are the essence of effective leadership, ensuring the path toward success remains illuminated and attainable.

THE ISTE STANDARDS

Chapter 4 explores several aspects of the ISTE Education Leader Standards, particularly focusing on the **Visionary Planner Standard (3.2)**, the **Empowering Leader Standard (3.3)**, and the **Systems Designer Standard (3.4)**. Aligning with Standard 3.2, this chapter provides practical guidance on crafting a road map, prioritizing resources wisely, and continuously evaluating and adjusting strategies. These actions mirror the process of engaging stakeholders in establishing a shared vision (3.2.a), collaboratively creating a strategic plan (3.2.b), and evaluating progress on the plan while making course corrections (3.2.c).

Additionally, the chapter content aligns with Standard 3.3 by emphasizing the importance of empowering educators, fostering a culture of innovation and collaboration, and supporting educators in using technology to meet diverse learning needs. This resonates with empowering educators to exercise professional agency (3.3.a), inspiring a culture of innovation (3.3.c), and supporting educators in using technology to advance learning (3.3.d).

Furthermore, the chapter reflects aspects of Standard 3.4 by emphasizing the need for effective communication, talent discovery, and continuous evaluation and adjustment. This corresponds to leading teams to establish robust infrastructure and systems (3.4.a), ensuring sufficient resources for supporting effective use of technology (3.4.b), and continually improving operations through partnerships (3.4.d).

Build the Skill of Reflection

Have you seen people repeatedly follow the same unsuccessful process, hoping for a better outcome each time they do it? Perhaps you have felt stuck in a similar loop and don't know how to get out. Conversely, you might know others who can somehow take all incoming information from a less-than-optimal situation and create a flaw-free "cleanup" that magically turns everything around and saves the project. How does that happen?

A highly effective Edtech Leader exercises the art of reflection. They can remove themselves from the situation they are mired in and reflect impassively on the issues, without making excuses. Because they are good reflectors, they get things done.

 ### KEY STRATEGIES

- Step back and review your actions, decisions, and outcomes. By reviewing your decision-making process and the results, you can identify areas of strength and any need for improvements.

- Learn from your positive and negative experiences. Lessons and insights from a certain project may apply to other issues you are dealing with.

- Use the art of reflection to learn about your leadership style, decision making, and critical-thinking skills. Use the reflective process to learn how you approach problems and clarify your values and beliefs.

- Reflection helps you explore your communication style and the impact your communication has as it supports the goals you are trying to achieve.

- Teach others how to be thoughtful reflectors. Doing a "talk-about" (when you talk through your reasoning), modeling reflection, and building reflective sessions into your team meetings helps to grow the art of reflection in others.

Here are some questions Savvy Edtech Leaders may ask themselves when they use their reflective muscle:

- *What worked well in the process?*

- *What didn't work well? Why didn't it?*

- *What were the factors that could have been changed?*

- *If somebody had altered them, would we have gotten closer to success?*

- *What are optimal conditions for success?*

- *What has worked well in the past, and how can I apply those successes to this situation?*

Once they have reviewed the issue, a great Edtech Leader will ask themselves: *What was my part in this situation that went poorly? What was my role in the success? What could I have done to help make the outcome better?* This part of the reflection takes great maturity, in that before we look at the external factors that may not have gone as well as we had planned, we first must look inside and hold ourselves accountable.

While there are many external factors that we cannot control, like weather, time, and other people's actions, what can we impact for the better? Is it cleaner and more transparent communication to all groups involved, or is it expectation management? Is it looking ahead and then working to mitigate the level of risk involved, or is it gathering more information from your stakeholders to better tailor your solution? Is it helping people name their fears so that you can help them build resiliency strategies? Or is it a simple rearrangement in the order of operations to get a more concise outcome?

A SAFE SPACE

I like to call areas of deficit the "gaps." When we use that word, we do not blame others; we just identify a gap between where something ended up and where we needed it to be. When we intentionally do not name the people involved and what they did wrong in the process, we provide a safe environment where team members can collaborate without feeling like they must be accurate one hundred percent of the time. We are human and sometimes do not get things right the first, second, or third time. You gain another nugget of knowledge every time you take the opportunity to try a new or innovative solution. What worked well? What didn't work well?

I often modeled the skill of continuous learning by talking through my lessons learned when working with my staff. While I made myself vulnerable, I wanted to model how to reflect and learn from past actions. I hoped others would pick up on the reflective method, learn to talk through problems, and collaborate to devise better solutions. By using this technique, I eventually saw others lower their aversion to risk, try new and innovative approaches, and then reflect upon them for a more well-rounded solution.

—DIANE DOERSCH

It may be human nature to shift accountability over to others for tasks or projects that did not go as planned. An astute Edtech Leader rises above the human instinct to place blame on individuals and instead uses their reflective skills and curiosity to home in on where the project may have started to go off track. They do not focus on what the team members did to cause the disconnect. Instead, they dig deep into the issue to discover the root causes. What was the cause of the problem? How could it have gone better?

Many times, things will go differently than planned, and there will be times when the outcomes turn out differently than you had hoped. Some might label the incident as a failure. As difficult as the word failure feels to a leader, it is a necessary opportunity to learn and grow. In reflection, one must accelerate the collection of information to establish best practices. For every "what didn't work," there is a "what will work." Identifying paths toward success often comes from the information learned from failures.

Helping Others Become Good Reflectors

Guiding others in the reflective process is one of the more complex tasks you may take on. Your modeling and "talk-abouts" will be essential in assisting others in developing their reflective skills. In fostering the growth of good reflectors, a Savvy Edtech Leader will be willing to step back and listen without creating conclusions or solutions for your thought partner. They must ask their own questions to help deepen their reflective processes.

Help your thought partner avoid defensiveness and excuses around where things went wrong. They need to remove themselves from the problem and work to identify root causes before they can see possible solutions. Modeling accountability for your actions and not naming others when discussing gaps helps keep focus on the problem, not the person.

Building Blocks for the Art of Reflection

Lead by example. Demonstrate the importance of reflection by engaging in reflective practices yourself. Share your learning experiences and do a talk-about to show your thought processes. Talk about how the art of reflection adds to your personal and professional development.

Set clear expectations. Let your team know that you expect large and small topic reflections as a part of daily work. They should be prepared to discuss those reflections with you as part of how your department does business.

Create a safe and supportive environment for review. Establish a culture where staff members can be open and honest in their reflections. Allowing your colleagues to voice their thoughts without defensiveness or judgment encourages an environment for collaboration.

Provide time for reflection. Reflection does not come naturally to all people. That is why modeling it, setting the expectation that examination will occur, and allowing thought to happen without judgment is essential. Be intentional about providing time for review so that people can dedicate their energy to their best thinking in the reflective process. They should think of the wins in their latest work, the challenges, and the lessons learned.

Hold regular meetings to provide feedback and guidance. Now that your team members have analyzed and successfully reflected, they need an opportunity to share their reflections. Create a time for sharing so people may share their thoughts and the lessons learned. It will help you understand what further support is needed and identify learning opportunities.

Encourage documentation. Encourage team members to document their reflections in writing. They can serve as historical markers and help them track growth in their thinking. With the creator's permission, they can be shared documents that can help further everybody's journey.

Building a standard procedure after small projects can also assist your colleagues in practicing the art of reflection. It doesn't have to be a long and complicated process; it could initially occur asynchronously and digitally. Have project participants fill out a shared plus/minus chart while everything is fresh in their memories. When you have time to talk in person, you may want to ask:

- Do you see any commonalities in the responses?

- What surprised you about the positives?

- Does anybody have more to share about them?

- Did anything surprise you about the negatives? (Watch here for people taking responsibility for shortcomings vs. blaming others.)

- Next time, what things would have to change?

- Was there more information we should have gathered or different perspectives to include?

- Is there data available that will help inform your decision?

- How could we have prevented some of the shortcomings?

- Do we have consistent patterns that lead to imperfections?

- Could we have used a different approach to our problem-solving methods?

- Were you able to effectively communicate your project to your audience?

- What should we have in place for people to succeed the next time we do a project?

While the art of reflection is important for you and your team, don't be too hard on yourselves! Acknowledging where the missteps took place and building a plan for what to do to prevent those unfortunate circumstances in the future is all you can do. Look at every gap as an opportunity to learn. Sometimes, success feels elusive, and you could get lost in your self-deprecating reflection. A Savvy Edtech Leader will know when to put the topic to rest.

Embrace Innovation

Innovation in edtech involves seeking unique ideas and solutions in technology's instructional, operational, or administrative uses in a K–12 environment. These innovative technology solutions should engage, assist, or challenge students and staff in new and more effective ways. Savvy Edtech Leaders can connect the dots in ways others may not see!

A creative person may think of a new way of doing something, but an innovator puts the idea into action. Authentic innovations require some failures along the way. You cannot innovate if you fear change. Calculated risks are required. Scary? Yes!

 KEY STRATEGIES

- Ensure innovative solutions are for problems or challenges that need solving.

- Do your homework and build from the ideas of others. Involve other department leaders, teachers, students, parents, and other stakeholders in the process.

- Create and communicate a road map and picture of success.

- Pilot the innovation within a smaller environment.

- Learn from mistakes that prevented initial success and take action to correct them.

Problems That Need Solving

Target innovative efforts at areas where conventional methods fall short or where new approaches could significantly enhance efficiency or effectiveness. The pursuit of innovation must be guided by a clear understanding of the challenge at hand, ensuring that resources, creativity, and expertise are channeled appropriately. Gather data and dig deep into the underlying causes of the problem. Talk to those actually affected.

Time and money are limited. Make a list of problems that require solutions. Use the information below to create a prioritized list that channels resources and expertise appropriately.

- Determine the time and human capital that you can allot to each problem.

- Determine the financial resources available.

- Work with an applicable team to determine which solutions will significantly impact the organization's stated goals.

- Narrow the list further by the level of urgency.

Know the difference between fact and opinion. In the edtech world, there are many opinions concerning what needs fixing.

Build from the Ideas of Others

Build off of the knowledge and experiences of others, including all stakeholders. Integrate various perspectives into the overall innovative solution. Talk with colleagues in your area, state, and country. Saving time saves money, and when you can build from an existing idea or process, it minimizes planning and startup time. Brainstorm with your team and encourage them to think outside the box and look at the challenge through different lenses. Don't think about only "what is" but lean into "what can be."

When we diligently research and gather information, we tap into a vast pool of knowledge accumulated by others. This enables us to build on their ideas, harness their experiences, and integrate various perspectives. Someone else's idea will often spark your creative and innovative juices.

A Road Map and Picture of Success

Many folks at any organization fear change and are comfortable with the familiar, even when the status quo is not efficient or effective. Edtech Leaders must cultivate buy-in. Envision the path ahead and vividly illustrate it to your team and others involved. Engage them in the creation, process, implementation, and evaluation of any innovations. Answer questions honestly.

Once a draft of the road map or plan has been determined, have a sample of stakeholders review the plan to make sure it is clear, concise, and doesn't have gaps in thinking. Develop a plan for communicating throughout the implementation.

Pilot the Innovation within a Smaller Environment

Piloting an innovative solution highlights potential issues with the advantages of limited exposure and minimal funds. A pilot ensures that any need for adjustments is exposed as the process unfolds. A smaller test environment simplifies the change process and allows for quick data collection to inform the need for ongoing tweaks or changes.

- Select a pilot group that reflects the larger environment where the innovation will be scaled.
- Communicate the road map and desired outcome to the pilot group.
- Solicit ongoing feedback.
- Make adjustments as needed.
- Provide ready support.

By implementing the innovation in a controlled and manageable setting, organizations can closely monitor its impact and performance without being overwhelmed by the complexities of a larger scale. This approach allows for real-time adjustments, quick identification of any challenges or bottlenecks, and fine-tuning processes.

Learn from Mistakes

Monitor progress throughout the implementation. With innovations, there will likely be mistakes or unintended consequences. Analyzing our errors paves the way for improvement. Mistakes provide us with invaluable lessons, offering insights into what went wrong and how to prevent similar mistakes in the future.

Edtech Leaders know there is no feeling more exhilarating than being presented with a challenge, seeing something others may not see, thinking through the idea, creating a plan, implementing the plan, and seeing positive results. Remember, every use of technology today was someone's innovative idea in the past.

Build Your Leadership Influence

Why does it matter if an Edtech Leader has leadership influence or builds it? Well, individuals are free to determine the dedication they bring to their work every day. Accomplished leaders comprehend that they must not rely solely on directive approaches to achieve effectiveness. The outdated "command and control" leadership style rarely yields success and often elicits resistance. As respected author, speaker, and leadership guru Kenneth Blanchard notes, "The pivotal element for prosperous leadership in today's world is influence, rather than authority."

 KEY STRATEGIES

- Embrace ambition on behalf of others. Influential Edtech Leaders foster ambitious goals for their employees, identifying and nurturing talents that individuals may not recognize in themselves. A key objective for an effective Edtech Leader is to help others achieve their highest potential.

- Blend autonomy and authority. Influential Edtech Leaders cultivate respect and motivation by balancing personal connection with their teams and encouraging their development through trust in their work quality, time management, and resourcefulness. Encouraging autonomy not only empowers individuals and teams but also fuels creativity, enhancing motivation and inspiration.

- Invest time in getting to know your team members. To effectively influence and align leaders with your vision, invest time in discovering their interests beyond work and building genuine connections.

- Establish trust and commitment with your team. To establish trust and commitment, Edtech Leaders must genuinely care for their employees, understand their key goals and values, and align them with the organizational vision.

- Build positive relationships with your employees. Building positive relationships with your team is crucial for effective leadership, even if it doesn't mean becoming best friends. By showing genuine interest, initiating conversations, and understanding your coworkers, you can enhance your leadership influence and improve workplace dynamics.

Gaining influence over an organization and its employees is not automatically bestowed upon acquiring a specific title, reaching a certain level of leadership or authority, or occupying a particular office. Genuine leadership lies in the power to influence, rather than relying solely on authority. Being a good Edtech Leader means being able to change the way others think and act. But this doesn't mean controlling or manipulating them. It's about understanding what makes your team want to do their best. How much your team trusts you is a big part of how much you can influence them. The more they trust you, the more you can shape their thoughts and actions. There are several ways great Edtech Leaders build that trust and influence.

Proving you're trustworthy is an excellent place to start. To earn people's trust, you need to show them you're a good person who knows what they're doing. Educator and author Stephen Covey noted there are four important parts to this:

- Honesty
- Making your motives clear
- Having the skills for your job
- Delivering on your promises

Covey also said that trust starts with trusting yourself and showing others they can trust you too. Once people see you're reliable, they'll begin to trust you, and you'll be able to influence them more.

Get others involved and make connections to help build your leadership influence. Being a leader isn't about doing everything yourself. Your team must be part of the process if you want to influence them. Get their opinions on big decisions that will impact them. Involve them early on when changes are being made. Try to understand what's important to them. If they see you care about their interests, they'll be more willing to follow your lead.

Be clear about what you expect, and hold people accountable. If you want your team to deliver outstanding results, you must tell them precisely what you expect and ensure everyone does their part. If you don't, your team won't trust you. This makes it harder for you to influence them positively.

Show your excitement. Being passionate about your work will energize your team. Passion is contagious and can't be faked. If you don't care about what you're doing, why should anyone else? People admire Edtech Leaders who can look ahead and get others excited about their vision. When you share your enthusiasm, you can influence your team to get behind your ideas.

Be open to others' influence. Influence should go both ways. One of the best ways to increase your influence is to show that you're willing to be influenced by others. Listen to their ideas, consider different viewpoints, and use their skills. When you show openness, your team will respect and trust you more, increasing your influence.

To inspire your employees to follow your guidance, showcasing your proficiency and demonstrating competence is crucial. Keep advancing your expertise and understanding in your field, and then share it with your team members to influence and empower them.

To sum it up, leadership is about positively influencing others. A Savvy Edtech Leader doesn't force their team to do things. Instead, they inspire their team to believe in the leader's vision and goals. When used correctly, influence can bring

---

LEADER CREATES LEADERS

When Sheryl Abshire made the leap from elementary librarianship to principalship, she had no previous administrative experience. As she began her lengthy leadership journey, she was determined to support other teachers who dreamed of a leadership journey of their own. As she observed and worked with teams of talented teachers, she knew that part of her role was to inspire these potential leaders to rise up and become the leaders they were destined to be. In her district more than twenty teachers she worked with became exceptional educational leaders in schools and at the district level. Her leadership influence continues today as she facilitates, coaches, and mentors hundreds of aspiring Edtech Leaders as a facilitator and leader in the CoSN Early Career K12 CTO Academy.

significant changes, as everyone works together towards the same goal. An Edtech Leader who can positively influence their team builds trust and pushes everyone toward excellence.

Influence a Winning Team

One of the main reasons people get hired for leadership roles is so they can build and influence a winning team. When Diane Doersch hired leaders for her department, she often asked candidates to provide examples of their leadership in their current or past job. Sometimes people would confuse being assigned additional tasks by their supervisor with being a leader. While something within them may have made them a good candidate for the extra tasks, doing additional work does not necessarily constitute leadership. Other candidates could talk about how they could identify talents on their team, focus on the project's goals, and help move all efforts in the same direction to complete the project. Those candidates displayed leadership. Leadership in your field involves effectively guiding and inspiring people to achieve your shared goals.

 KEY STRATEGIES

- Before striving to influence others, you must feel confident and competent as a leader. Start from within to build your leadership skills.

- Others are watching you and your leadership style. Welcome discourse and take in different perspectives. There is nothing wrong with a leader changing their mind after gaining further information.

- Model integrity and competence confidently so others can see what they want to become.

- Your positive attitude is contagious, even during the most difficult of times. More than knowledge or power, your positive energy will be what is remembered and may serve as the critical factor that helps get your team to the finish line.

- Take time to celebrate, not just at the end of a project but along the way as well. When people feel appreciated, they will recommit to their goals and find the energy to get things done.

Influential Edtech Leaders who can inspire a winning team have qualities that set them apart. They may have a way of looking toward the future. They understand what it takes to improve the organization and move toward the vision. They can share the vision with their team to inspire the group to work in that direction. They foster a positive work environment where everybody's voice and viewpoints are considered.

How can you be an influential leader? The first thing is to examine yourself and your leadership skills before you can work to be effective.

Do a self-assessment of your leadership skills. What are your strengths, and where do you see gaps? You could seek colleagues' feedback or seek professional development on leadership to gain insight into your leadership style.

Ensure that you are always learning. What are the latest trends in your field? What's going on outside your field and what dots might you connect? What are other leaders concerned about, and what are they placing on the back burner? Attending conferences, participating in webinars, and reading trade publications can help build your general knowledge in and outside your field.

Seek out a thought partner. Discussing the challenges of your profession with this thought partner, someone with whom you can exchange ideas and who can help you navigate a situation, will help to grow your perspectives and understand more deeply the intricacies of the leadership landscape. Regularly talking with the thought partner will ensure that you hit timely topics as they arise in your work environment.

Build a robust collaborative network. Join professional associations, attend industry conferences, and participate in collaborative opportunities within your network. Being a contributing team member within your professional circles helps you to build your brand and reputation as a go-to leader.

Embrace new challenges. Working in the IT field means things change rapidly. It is essential to keep up with the latest trends. Avoiding these challenges will not help your department advance.

Take leadership training. Home in on the specific topics where you notice gaps in your leadership. Such training could include team building, change management, effective communication, making data-informed decisions, and problem-solving.

Reflect and adapt. Build the art of reflection into everything you do, and help your team learn to reflect as well. What worked well? Where did you notice gaps? What will your team do next time to avoid those gaps from happening?

Take on a positive outlook. Displaying loyalty to others and taking the "glass half full" approach in the direst of circumstances can provide hope and a rejuvenation of efforts to get the job done. Celebrating the small steps, being grateful for the efforts to get a project to its current state, and being unwavering in meeting goals will be contagious.

Lead by example. Your team is watching what you do. Demonstrate the leadership skills you would like to see in your collaborative cadre, and remember that no work is beneath you. You should not ask others to do things that you would not do. Show integrity, professionalism, and a positive attitude at all times.

LEAD BY EXAMPLE

I recall handling a challenging, emotionally-charged IT team meeting. Afterward, one of our department members followed me to my office and wanted to discuss how I handled the situation. When the time for difficult conversations came in the meeting, she reviewed what she would do if she were in a leadership situation. The curious staff member said, "You handled it calmly and didn't get rattled. What made you do and say the things you did?" I noted that this was a highly observant employee who watches, learns, applies, and reflects. It reminded me that our teams learn from their leaders every day, good or bad; they are always watching. Leading by example lets you influence your winning team.

— DIANE DOERSCH

Following are some other things can you do to influence your team:

Develop a clear vision. Always work to help your team understand the why. Develop a clear vision for your team so they know what is expected. Ensure that you support your team, and let them know your expectation of what a completed project looks like. Tie the department goal to your organization's purpose, so your team understands that their work advances your whole organization.

Encourage individual growth. Support your team members' requests for professional learning for personal development. Creating a learning culture will lower the barriers to your staff asking for learning opportunities. Build new knowledge into your monthly meetings, so your team learns something new monthly, and share external learning opportunities with them. Model your professional learning and admit where you see growth areas in yourself.

Foster teamwork. We are all better together. Encourage collaboration and the sharing of knowledge so that everybody improves. Model teamwork with other departments and build partnerships into your expectations for your entire department. Bring organizational values forward, such as transparency, commitment to the team and goals, and continuous improvement. Cross-training prevents bottlenecks in tasks so that when one person is not present at work, your department's business can continue.

Provide feedback and recognition. Regularly providing feedback is a very impactful way of influencing your team members. You can influence your managers by regularly meeting with them individually, by serving as a thought partner, and by understanding the barriers to their projects so that you can help remove them. Encourage innovation and creativity in their work. Having tough conversations about any gaps you see becomes easier when you have regular check-ins. Trust will be built, and vulnerabilities will be uncovered. Those are all ingredients for a trusting relationship that lends itself to friendly feedback and continuous improvement.

Delegate and empower. As team members grow their competencies, there will be opportunities for them to receive delegated work. Provide a safe space for your staff with new delegations to ask questions and receive frequent feedback so that they feel confident that they are on track. Empower them with the tools and resources needed to complete the new task, and give them a clear picture of a completed project.

Manage conflicts effectively. Always encourage people with disagreements to speak to each other first before raising the issue to a supervisor's level. Team members must take the opportunity to work conflict out themselves first. If you need to intervene, encourage diplomatic honesty, and always focus on the goals and not the people. Using this approach will assist in guiding team members through conflict. Do not allow people to run from tough conversations; instead, thoughtfully provide them the support they need to work through disagreements.

Celebrate successes. Your team members need to know they are making progress. Use your regular meeting to celebrate individual achievements. Build a culture of praise and sharing so that team members report to you when they or their colleagues have accomplished a goal. A Savvy Edtech Leader always gets permission before highlighting individual accomplishments in front of others. Not everybody celebrates the same. Some employees may want their names announced out loud, while others may appreciate a personal acknowledgment of a job well done through a handwritten note or encouraging email.

Influencing a winning team means that you have consistently built your leadership skills and can now support and impact your team purposefully.

Proceed with Intention and Navigate with Purpose

Proceeding with intention as a department or organization's Edtech Leader requires establishing a long-term vision that aligns with the organization's goals and core values, and developing a strategic plan. As Edtech Leaders, we develop strategic plans for procuring, managing, securing, and using technology resources, always planning with equity and sustainability in mind.

This process requires the engagement of a cross section of stakeholders. Collaboration with these stakeholders ensures that their perspectives and needs are considered when setting goals and objectives. It is critical that Edtech Leaders collaborate both horizontally and vertically within the K–12 ecosystem to meet the needs and understand the challenges of everyone we serve.

The contents of a strategic plan include goals and objectives, strategies to reach the goal, professional development needs, and resource allocations. An evaluation process to measure progress toward achieving the goals must be established. Each new initiative or planned action should be tied to one or more of the established goals as a strategy for an objective. Include preliminary documents, charts, rubrics, evaluation instruments, and other data sources in the appendixes if appropriate.

 ### KEY STRATEGIES

- Collect data from various sources. Evaluate what you have to determine what you need. Use qualitative and quantitative methods to comprehensively understand the current situation.

- Engage a cross section of stakeholders. Work with all district departments as well as representatives from schools, student bodies, and the communities served.

- Develop the Strategic Plan with major goals and measurable and time-bound objectives.

- Evaluate and make adjustments as needed.

Collect Data from Various Sources

Data sources include surveys, inventories, interviews, focus groups, research, existing documents or reports, and internal data analysis. Familiarize yourself with any organization and department procedures and policies that can affect your work.

A needs assessment is crucial to understanding the specific requirements and challenges of the organization and the technology resources needed. This assessment helps identify areas where modifications or changes can positively impact and inform the goals and objectives in the plan. Look at the results of any needs assessment through multiple lenses. After reviewing the needs assessments and other available data, do a SWOT (Strengths, Weaknesses, Opportunities, and Threats) analysis. Identify strengths and weaknesses (S-W) and broader opportunities and threats (O-T).

Previous budgets or financial printouts often show trends and cycles for spending. Note patterns and be prepared to move quickly when funds are available.

Secure current and comprehensive inventories of available staff and resources.

Edtech Leaders are often caught between internal and external factors. We often must rely on external workers, vendors, and stakeholders. Yet, our practices, systems, and processes are designed for those working within the organization. Reconciling the two is an ongoing challenge, and both must be considered when developing a strategic plan. Create an inventory of everyone who must be considered in your planning.

Look for gaps between the current state and desired outcomes. This analysis will help determine the most critical areas to address in the strategic plan. Involve stakeholders in the needs assessment process to ensure their perspectives are considered. Engagement fosters buy-in for the strategic plan.

Develop the Strategic Plan

A strategic plan should be a living document. Write it so that it will not be outdated before you can share it! Your goals and objectives should be specific, measurable, achievable, relevant, and time-bound (SMART). Add action steps, timelines, and resource allocations. The following steps are a simplified guide for a first draft.

The needs assessment will have identified areas for improvement in services, access, safety, learning, and other aspects for current and potential future stakeholders. The results should be used to develop more effective action plans. Start by establishing benchmarks. Using your SWOT analysis, formulate specific statements that keep track of your advancement in reaching your goals and objectives. For instance, perhaps the current status shows that eighty percent of all users can access digital resources both onsite and from home. If your objective is one hundred percent access, you can track the percentage of users without access and easily report progress.

When developing a strategic plan, it is crucial to effectively utilize goals, objectives, actions, resource allocation, and data sources. The following nine tips are not all-inclusive but can serve as a guide to get started.

1. Create SMART goals to provide your strategic plan's overarching direction and purpose. They represent the broad outcomes your department aims to achieve.

2. Write objectives as specific and measurable targets that contribute to accomplishing the established goals. Objectives help break down the goals into actionable steps.

3. Develop actions or concrete tasks or initiatives that will be implemented to achieve the objectives. They should be clearly defined, time-bound, and assigned to responsible individuals or teams.

4. Determine and allocate resources, such as budget, personnel, and equipment, to support implementation of the actions. This step requires careful consideration of priorities and ensuring that resources are allocated efficiently and effectively. If funding is not currently available, but the actions are necessary for success, note the actions as "Unfunded." This documentation can serve as a "need" when funding becomes available, or it can entice other departments to shift funds to support an objective that is beneficial to their department.

5. Document the data sources that support the why. for actions. These sources include internal data from surveys, evaluations, observations, stakeholder feedback, industry trends, and best practices.

6. Professional development may be an integral piece of your strategic plan as it is crucial in enhancing your team's knowledge, skills, and competencies. By investing in professional development initiatives, you ensure that your people remain current with industry trends, best practices, and emerging technologies while fostering continuous learning and growth. Professional

development initiatives can encompass a wide range of activities, including training programs, workshops, conferences, mentoring, coaching, and educational opportunities.

7. Appendixes are like friendly companions providing organized documents to support your strategy. Appendixes help clarify the information in the rest of the plan, so you don't have to go on a side trip to find credentials and evidence. To make your strategic plan concise and easy to read and understand, avoid taking a detour into the weeds in the body of the plan. In the digital version, link to documents in the appendixes when applicable.

8. A budget summary should be included in the plan. Often a comprehensive budget is part of the appendixes. The budget may include quantities, descriptions, unit costs, totals, funding numbers, and funding sources.

9. An executive summary provides a quick overview of your entire plan. Its purpose is to provide a snapshot of the key elements and highlights of the strategic plan in a clear and engaging manner. Include a brief description of the department's mission, vision, and goals, along with the leading strategies and initiatives or actions that will be implemented to achieve them. You may also include a summary of the landscape and key elements from the SWOT analysis.

Evaluate and Make Adjustments

Set benchmarks, monitor progress, and communicate successes. Regularly evaluate the effectiveness and impact of your department's work. Establish metrics and evaluation frameworks to assess the progress toward reaching goals and meeting objectives. Make data-driven decisions to refine strategies.

Staying informed about emerging technologies, research, and best practices is essential to leading with intention. By following these key strategies and developing a comprehensive data-driven strategic plan, you can lead intentionally, ensuring your direction is purposeful, effective, equitable, and sustainable.

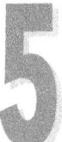

Crystal Clear Leadership
The Power of Transparency in Edtech

In today's world, performance expectations are the bedrock of a flourishing organizational culture. These expectations are not mere checklists or traditional job descriptions; they are a blend of behaviors, attitudes, and actions that embody and enhance an organization's vision, mission, and core values. Successful Edtech Leaders transcend ordinary leadership by meticulously outlining these expectations, creating an environment where trust, brand representation, and mutual commitment thrive. By collaborating with key leaders and high performers, these visionary leaders craft a culture where expectations are transparent, and examples of high performance are celebrated.

It's imperative for leaders in educational technology to embrace and champion transparency. The ability to communicate with clarity and integrity is not only admired but also expected in our increasingly transparent world. Edtech Leaders must harness this paradigm, turning transparency into a strategic advantage for themselves and their organizations (Lynch, 2023).

THE ISTE STANDARDS

This chapter's emphasis on transparency and performance expectations aligns closely with the **Empowering Leader Standard (3.3)** and the **Visionary Planner Standard (3.2)** from the ISTE Education Leader Standards. These standards underscore the significance of clear, transparent leadership in educational technology settings.

The Empowering Leader Standard highlights the importance of creating a culture where educators and learners are encouraged to use technology innovatively. This standard supports this chapter's focus on setting clear performance expectations, fostering trust, and empowering team members by promoting knowledge sharing and delegation. This empowerment allows for a robust, transparent environment where leadership and team member roles are clear, promoting operational efficiency and reducing burnout.

The Visionary Planner Standard involves engaging stakeholders in developing a shared vision for technology use that enhances learning outcomes. This planning and strategic vision are crucial in setting performance expectations that are aligned with the organization's goals. By ensuring that these expectations are clearly communicated and integrated into the organizational culture, leaders can use transparency as a strategic tool, making it easier for team members to align with the organizational vision and values.

Both standards advocate for a leadership approach that is not only clear and direct but also inclusive and supportive, enabling team members to excel and embody the organization's values and goals effectively.

Such leaders also recognize the limitations of being indispensable. While possessing unique skills can seem advantageous, it can also lead to operational bottlenecks and personal burnout. Exceptional Edtech Leaders strategically delegate, ensuring knowledge redundancy and empowering others to step into roles of significance. Furthermore, they epitomize the essence of positive role models. To paraphrase philosopher Albert Schweitzer, "Setting an example is not the main means of influencing others; it is the only means." By being self-aware, maintaining a professional demeanor, and displaying genuine respect for others, they set the gold standard for leadership and inspire a culture of continuous growth, mutual respect, and unwavering commitment to excellence.

Performance expectations are the behaviors, attitudes, and actions that describe how we expect team members to perform their jobs and interact with others. Performance expectations go beyond job descriptions because they have common principles that reinforce the organization's vision, purpose, beliefs, values, and brand.

How do we set performance expectations? Set the organization up for success by describing the following:

- How do you expect employees to develop trusting relationships?

- How do you expect employees to behave?

- How do you expect employees to demonstrate the organization's values?

- How do you expect employees to represent your brand?

- How can employees expect you to do the same?

Go Beyond Mere Job Descriptions

Employee behavior can be challenging to explain, so you must describe what you expect methodically. These expectations are the core of the culture. Outline your expectations and ask your key leaders and high performers to share specific examples of organizational attributes that would demonstrate a high-performing culture. Use your vision, mission, beliefs, values, and brand as the guide.

 ### *KEY STRATEGIES*

- Incorporate performance expectations into daily discussions, ensuring they are highlighted in every communication. Celebrate successes by using specific examples to illustrate when expectations are exceeded, like praising a technician who swiftly resolves a teacher's technical issue. Use detailed praise, such as acknowledging how a technician's quick action allowed a student to access necessary information for homework, reinforcing the value of their exceptional service.

- When performance falls short of expectations, address it directly in everyday conversations. For instance, if a team member fails to follow through on a commitment, express your disappointment clearly: "You promised the teacher her laptop by Friday to prepare for the weekend,

and I'm concerned about how she managed her work without it."
Highlight the impact of their actions, questioning how the teacher and
her students coped with the unmet commitment.

- Use performance expectations as the basis for recognition. Be
  intentional about any recognition. Tie every recognition to what is
  important, and be specific in the recognition so the desired behavior,
  attitudes, and actions support your expectations.

- Establish clear performance expectations in every employee evaluation,
  going beyond standard assessments. Incorporate a dedicated section
  within the evaluations that specifically addresses how well performance expectations are met. Commit to the necessary documentation
  and engage in crucial conversations that reinforce these expectations.

- Be an example in every action you take and decision you make. If you
  cannot model the performance expectations set forth for the organization, pack up and get out. There is no room for dispute.

Values shape the organization's culture and reflect what is essential, so start by
describing the desired behaviors, attitudes, and actions that support your core
values. One easy way to dive in is to set the performance expectations for each
value category. For example, using the core value of TRUST (Talented, Reliable,
Ubiquitous, Student Focused, and Transparent), explain the meaning of the
performance expectations as they relate to each value category, so expectations are
clearly understood.

Following are specific examples of performance expectations aligning to the core
values of TRUST. These examples are personal and meant to reflect the culture you
seek to build.

Talented. Possess advanced technical, academic, and interpersonal skills with
the capacity to lead, solve problems, serve, innovate, and grow. Keep skills
current and master new technical knowledge and skills. Participate in trade
and professional organizations to acquire advanced technical skills. Seek out
experts and involve others who have more significant experience and expertise.
Take responsibility for learning and actively pursue growth opportunities.
Find innovative solutions by using creativity and thinking outside the box
when providing solutions. Build social networks with other professionals to
collaborate and share information and ideas. Find mentors who can assist in

delivering more challenging experiences that lead to more significant roles and responsibilities. Challenge the status quo by asking, "Why not?" Read, listen, watch for trends, and proactively transfer new knowledge and information to others. Obtain increasing levels of certifications, education, and professional development.

Reliable. Demonstrate consistent performance by being dependable and trustworthy in all interactions. Address all customer and employee communications within the same business day. Balance competing priorities using effective time management solutions. Use follow-up communication if commitments still need to be met. Focus on understanding all customer requests. Be professionally approachable and welcome questions. Gain trust by being available, honest, and authentic. Perform the hard work that is required. Serve in a caring, enthusiastic, and friendly way. Acknowledge limitations and provide alternatives. Establish clear-cut agreements and set realistic expectations.

Ubiquitous. Sustain widespread ability to connect and use technology everywhere and anytime, seamlessly and safely. Weave technology into every aspect of work, education, and service. Create an interconnected environment where technology is indistinguishable from any other utility or activity. Eliminate concerns and perceptions of risk. The technology is safe, inappropriate access to information is blocked, and data is secure. Assured technology is optimally connected at maximum speeds. Be proactive. Monitor and predict issues before any need is recognized or problem occurs. Deliver integrated systems and technologies that interact in new and innovative ways. Sustain context-aware technologies that recognize customer needs and preferences in advance. Optimize success by integrating technology services across systems, platforms, devices, and applications to access and exchange data for sustained connectivity. Do whatever is possible to guarantee technology is available one hundred percent of the time. Make the technological experience easy, delightful, and stress free.

Student focused. Provide innovative learning opportunities that enhance students' capabilities through a rich, collaborative, and engaging education technology experience. Find ingenious ways to connect all students, all the time, outside the school's walls. Promote technologies that offer high student engagement (challenging, fun, engaging, and relevant to their age group and abilities). Seek technologies that provide multiple assessment forms, feedback, and learning methods. Actively engage with educators to understand what is needed to improve student support. Embrace the newest technologies to provide new opportunities for student learning. Help educators save time so they can focus on student learning. Place technology devices in the hands of all students so there are equitable opportunities for every student to dream and take responsibility for their learning.

Transparent. Serve authentically, free from pretense, and in a transparent and trustworthy manner. Share information by openly communicating issues, changes, limitations, and alternatives. Explain any service issue. Use affirmative language that is expressed in a positive tone to explain issues. Be vulnerable by demonstrating your desire to improve, grow, and learn from students and educators. Gather information and options in advance before drawing conclusions or formulating opinions. Acknowledge mistakes and shortcomings and seek to improve. Apologize when needed and be willing to apologize first in the spirit of teamwork. Be ready to modify plans in response to needs or changing directions. Tackle issues head-on by being action-oriented and results-driven. Give credit to others and show gratefulness for the opportunity to serve students, educators, and customers.

Thriving Edtech Leaders must define performance expectations and how they support the organizational culture. Employees must understand acceptable and unacceptable behaviors and expectations. There should be no room left for interpretation.

Delegate and Move Up

Have you ever felt that you should be cloned or duplicated? You possess skills and abilities that others in your organization do not have. While you may think that you have an advantage because your skills are in high demand, what happens when the work in your specified field becomes too great? Backups may occur because you are too busy. It may become challenging for you to meet deadlines. You will become more prone to burnout. This can lead to mental fatigue and a decline in physical well-being. If you are the sole possessor of the knowledge it takes to complete a complicated task, the opportunities to take time off are few because work needs you. It is impossible to scale projects dependent on your work because there is only one you, and you cannot promptly complete all the work. These are all signs that it's time to begin to delegate some of the work you do. As a result, you may move up.

KEY STRATEGIES

- It's difficult to be the only person in your team who is able to do a task or execute a process. Build capacity in others to share the work, and build opportunities for cross-training.

- Delegate work; it is healthy for your department and shows maturity in leadership.

- Spend significant time considering to whom you should delegate tasks. There may be several team members who are good candidates and eager for the opportunity.

- Provide learning opportunities and ongoing support so that trainees grow in the task and in confidence.

- Ensure you are providing ongoing support for the growth of your new delegate.

While delegating your tasks to others sounds daunting, cross-training is very important. If you tend to do everything yourself due to control issues or perfectionism, now is the time to think in a new strategic way. Training someone else in one of your areas of expertise with build capacity within your team.

Delegating work helps you better understand your teammates. Understanding their skills, experiences, and career aspirations allows you to find the best tasks for their talents. It also allows you to uncover their growth areas, placing them in assignments that help them stretch.

When you delegate, you allow your staff members to grow in a safe place. Your feedback and guidance are vital in helping them feel more confident in their work. The learning experience you personally provide to them fosters a learning culture and can allow for innovation.

By delegating, you provide leadership opportunities for aspiring leaders by giving them the autonomy to gather information, make decisions, solve problems, and take responsibility for a project. Leading a task or project also allows your team member to receive feedback, praise, and criticism so the project continually improves.

One of the incidental benefits of delegating work to others is that you may rise in the organization. When you build capacity behind you so that your team members can do the work you once did, you create time and space to participate in the organization at higher levels. By carefully selecting members of your team to do the tasks you once did, you become known for helping others learn. The organization will begin to see that you have the backs of your team members and have trained them to produce the same high-quality work you are known for. Having multiple people who can do your work allows you to move up the ladder because you are building a team of leaders behind you.

When you are thinking about delegating a task to others, there are many things you should consider:

How complex is the task? Assess the mission's complexity to evaluate whether it is appropriate for you to delegate. Does the job require specialized knowledge, expertise, or decision-making authority? Complex tasks may need careful consideration.

Does the task require special knowledge and abilities? Understand the skills, strengths, and capabilities of your team members. Match the task to the individual's skills and developmental needs to ensure they have the necessary knowledge and resources.

Does the trainee have the time to do it? People have full plates. Perhaps you can reassign some duties to allow the trainee to take on the proposed new task.

Do you have time to provide guidance and support? You are the only one who can confidently ensure your designee has the knowledge, skills, and disposition to do the job well. Be available to answer questions, advise, and help as a thought partner. Encourage them to be independent in their thinking but seek help when required.

A strategic leader works to build within their team with opportunities for cross-training. Delegating tasks allows multiple people to share knowledge and take ownership. It creates a culture of collaboration, increases team productivity, and identifies next possible department leaders.

When you consider who on your team you are going to delegate tasks to, here are things to consider:

Define the project's key requirements. What are the requirements and qualifications necessary to lead the task or project? Think about communication skills, technical skills, and experience. Create a clear profile of what you are looking for in a team member before identifying somebody to take on the task.

Review your candidates. Look for people who have not only some of the skills and knowledge but also those who show great potential and desire to be a continuous learner.

Provide learning opportunities. Use the talk-about method when you reason through some of your regular work so that your team can follow your thinking and contribute to the work. Invite people to volunteer for small work teams. Share and support outside professional learning opportunities.

Gather feedback from colleagues, team members, and end users. Ask about the potential delegate's performance, capabilities, and potential for growth to gauge whether they may be a good fit.

Gauge the candidate's readiness. You can assign tasks that become increasingly difficult to assess decision-making skills under pressure and the ability to communicate changes and progress to others.

Ultimately, you will find that when you build capacity in others to do some leadership tasks, you can devote more time to strategic planning for the organization. Your influence will grow, and you will find that you move up and advance because you have many competent people behind you who can pick up the work.

Lead by Example

A professional role model is an individual others look up to, admire, and emulate in the work environment. We all know individuals who stand out as role models—beacons of inspiration, integrity, and leadership. Edtech Leaders who are role models are typically committed to continuous learning and self-improvement while maintaining humility and respect toward others. Leading by example may not be the only means, but it is undoubtedly one of the best ways to motivate others to strive to be their best.

To serve as a role model, you must go beyond caring about your own personal success; you must care about the success of others and have a positive impact on them. Edtech Leaders who serve as positive role models are self-aware, positive people with humility and empathy for others. They are professional and of high integrity. They own their mistakes and actively seek ways to correct them. When a leader demonstrates accountability, others will often follow. Model authentic respect for other people and for different ideas. An influential role model has achieved a healthy work-life balance and is optimistic and confident but never arrogant.

 KEY STRATEGIES

- Set high standards and exemplify professionalism and integrity. Always be aware of your actions and attitudes. Strive to be confident, humble, positive, optimistic, self-aware, and empathetic with others.

- Generously share knowledge as a thought partner, mentor, or coach to others, and guide others on their path to success.

- Demonstrate continuous learning and adaptability. Stay informed about the latest edtech trends, innovations, and developments.

- Promote collaboration, build relationships, and create an inclusive environment within your department, organization, and professional community.

Exemplify Professionalism and Integrity

You may not be aware, but as an Edtech Leader, the people on your team, in your organization, and in your professional orbit are influenced by you. They may try to emulate you. It is essential to set high standards for yourself and consistently exemplify professionalism. Your actions and the quality of your work should be examples of excellence.

Professionalism is paramount in every interaction. Maintain a positive attitude and exemplary work ethic that serve as a model for others. A professional appearance suited to the work environment reinforces credibility and garners respect. Integral to professionalism is staying true to your values, practicing honesty, and consistently delivering on commitments. Inclusivity must also guide actions and communication, ensuring all voices are heard and valued in pursuing collective goals.

Generously Share Knowledge

Sharing your knowledge can be a sticky wicket. Read the room! Ensure that others are actively seeking your ideas and thoughts and will welcome guidance. Sharing is not a one-way conversation. Consider being a thought partner as opposed to "the expert." Be open to sharing your knowledge and experiences. When appropriate, offer guidance, advice, and insights to help others grow and achieve their goals. Actively seek opportunities to partner with aspiring professionals in edtech. When engaged in a conversation where someone is seeking your opinion, have empathy and avoid minimizing the problem.

Demonstrate Continuous Learning and Adaptability

To be a role model, you must embrace a mindset of continuous learning and adaptability. You should stay updated with industry trends and be open to change. Engage in continuous learning through professional development activities and organizations. Attend conferences and workshops or pursue advanced education to expand your knowledge. Read relevant white papers, articles, and books.

Promote Collaboration and Build Relationships

Effective Edtech Leaders actively encourage a culture of knowledge sharing and collaboration. They collaborate with others, leveraging each other's strengths to achieve common goals. Actively network and build relationships with other professionals in your field, on your team, and within your school system. Participate in industry events, engage in professional associations, and connect with both like-minded individuals and those who offer a different perspective.

6

Catalysts of Change
Building and Inspiring Dynamic Teams

Have you ever seen an extraordinary leader in action and thought, "Wow, they are really good at what they do; how can I be like them?" Leadership researchers Brykman and King state, "Leaders who encourage their employees to learn on the job and speak up with ideas and suggestions for change have teams that are more effective and resilient in the face of unexpected situations" (2021).

This chapter discusses some of the "extra" qualities you may have had difficulty identifying. We talk about how leaders can help their team members' visions become reality. We explore how to balance focusing on the future while performing well today. We discuss the importance of finding the right people to coach and elevate to create real organizational change. Leaders can leverage their work by diversifying their team and knowledge base. A good Edtech Leader can jigsaw all the team's talents together into one dynamic force that gets the job done.

Focus on the Small Things

Don't discount the importance of "the small things" in creating a healthy work environment. Don't ignore your own health or that of your team. Be kind and show gratitude. Learn something new every day.

 KEY STRATEGIES

- Be intentional about the image of yourself, your department, and the work that you do. Every aspect, from your personal demeanor to the services your department produces, should align with the desired perception.

- Agreed-upon norms for how people should communicate their ideas, disagree, and conduct themselves in meetings help everyone feel safe and involved. These norms should be clearly and constantly communicated.

- Establish and maintain a current and positive professional online presence. Refrain from posting negative comments, personal opinions, or beliefs that conflict with the district's core values.

- Before publicizing information, ensure its accuracy and that it communicates the intended message. This process involves thorough fact-checking, consideration of potential implications, and alignment with overarching communication objectives.

- Present a unified message. Those outside the team view any message from a team member as representative of the entire team.

Maintain a Positive Image

When we first meet someone, we form an opinion about them. Even as we get to know them better, it isn't easy to modify that initial opinion. It takes seconds for an impression to be made but perhaps years to change it. Always present the best you.

- **Make eye contact.** Look directly into the eyes of your discussion partner. Normal eye contact shows you hear what the other person is saying and are interested. When speaking, eye contact implies that you are confident in what you are saying and truthful. Remember to blink!

- **Smile.** A sincere smile shows interest, confidence, and approachability. Be aware of your "resting" facial expression even when you don't think anyone is looking.

- **Dress appropriately for the profession.** Clean, neat clothing appropriate for the profession is essential during interviews and when meeting with the leadership team, superintendent, and board. Proper attire can boost your confidence and perception of yourself. Model the professionalism you want to see in your team members.

Be true to your values and beliefs, and be transparent about your motives, even under pressure. There are ways to respectfully disagree or express your opinions. When communicating with someone in a higher position, acknowledge their position and ask if it is the appropriate time to provide a different point of view.

Be a prepared communicator. Being a good communicator means doing your homework, being clear and concise, and having empathy when delivering unpleasant news. A good communicator is also an attentive, interested listener.

Honor Other People's Time

Edtech Leaders must be careful not to underestimate how much time it will take to accomplish a task. Often, emergencies or unplanned events take precedence over scheduled work. The end result is that most of us have more to do than we have time to do it! A good rule of thumb is to under-commit and over-deliver.

If you can't attend a meeting or will be late, let the people expecting you know as soon as possible. Try to call or text if possible; emails may not be checked in time. Check the schedules of your team members who may be involved before committing their time. When scheduling a meeting, inform the involved parties of the expected duration. Make every effort to start and end meetings on time.

Maintain a Positive Professional Online Presence

In today's environment, Edtech Leaders should maintain an online presence as part of their professional networking efforts.

Separate your personal and professional online accounts. Use platforms that are best suited for your profession. Be intentional about whom you connect with, and network, network, network.

Be intentional about what you share. Anything you post could be quoted. Avoid online rants. In today's interconnected world, maintaining a levelheaded and composed online presence is crucial for career growth and networking.

Ensure that your professional profile picture, biography, and employment details are current. Verify that all posted content is current, accurate, and engaging.

Ensure Accuracy

Precision in decimal point placement is essential; an error could be disastrous. An errant autocorrect can cause a public uproar!

Edtech Leaders deal daily with budgets, measurements, quantities, and other precise numbers. Read and record numbers carefully. Double-check calculations to ensure all columns balance. Stand back, look at the total, and ask yourself if the result aligns with your expectations.

Proofread everything, including emails, texts, notes, documentation, professional social media posts, and web posts, before pressing Send. Ensure the message is clear and concise and leaves no room for misinterpretation. Consider having a proofreading buddy.

Present a Clear and Unified Message

It is vital that everyone in your department presents a unified message concerning any project, timeline, process, or practice before it goes public with the entire learning community. A unified message from your department or team serves as a cornerstone for instilling confidence in you and your team. Prioritize providing well-thought-out, clear, and concise responses, fostering understanding and trust among stakeholders. Transparency remains non-negotiable; we believe in openly sharing information to maintain integrity and credibility. Pre-meetings with team members ahead of larger discussions enable alignment, while post-meeting summaries ensure clarity and accountability.

Focusing on the little things every day helps effective Edtech Leaders create a culture of excellence, attention to detail, trust, confidence, and continuous improvement, all of which are essential for success. Even something as simple as a handwritten note to show gratitude or building a few minutes for celebrations into your team meetings can make a huge difference in the culture of your department or organization.

"Multiply" Your Leadership

Do you have the knowledge and leadership skills to help others improve their talents and contribute to their growth?

Successful Edtech Leaders create leadership potential in other staff members. They understand the power of multiplying their organization's growth by transforming their key followers into leaders. When a leader can only directly influence the organization's growth through the people with whom they interact, their impact is limited to those individuals. However, when you develop a leader, you can influence and impact many more people within your organization. Your goal as a Savvy Edtech Leader is to multiply the number of people you interact with. It only makes sense to work diligently to create a leader from a follower, expanding your influence and significantly contributing to your organization's growth.

It is crucial to develop leaders who can think ahead and take decisive action, particularly in crisis situations such as the COVID-19 pandemic. Insights from Wharton management professor Mike Useem and former General Electric CEO Jack Welch, emphasizing continuous learning and the development of leadership talent throughout an organization, provide comprehensive insights into the real-world applications of the principle that true leaders focus on creating more leaders rather than followers (Wharton Executive Education, 2020).

KEY STRATEGIES

- Develop others' leadership skills. Successful leaders understand that their organization's growth can be advanced by transforming key followers into leaders.

- Create a leadership training program. Identify and recruit potential leaders—those characterized by positivity, loyalty, self-improvement, and creativity—for specialized leadership training.

- Foster a positive work environment. Create an environment that nurtures leadership development, offers new responsibilities, and empowers decision-making and achievement.

- Exemplify leadership traits. Display accountability and gratitude, celebrate successes, lead with purpose, cultivate kindness, provide clear direction, focus on mentoring, and enable problem-solving.

- Promote continuous improvement. Even after the previous steps are implemented, a multiplying leader should continually provide feedback and adapt to the evolving needs of their team and organization, while also seeking advanced leadership training and opportunities for delegation.

Think about the following outcomes when you invest time working with your team. If you only focus on the bottom twenty percent, you'll spend time improving their weaknesses. However, when you work one-on-one with your strongest followers, your team with the most potential, you can enhance their strengths. By investing time in teaching your top followers leadership skills, you indirectly affect every person they interact with. That's a powerful impact for a leader.

To be identified as a multiplying leader, you should develop and be known for the following seven characteristics:

1. **Takes Accountability.** A multiplying leader embodies accountability by owning their actions and impact on the team. They admit and learn from mistakes, seek feedback, and are open to criticism. They also hold their team accountable by setting clear expectations and standards. Leading by example, they promote a culture of accountability, which is crucial for individual and organizational growth.

2. **Practices Gratitude and Celebrates Wins.** A multiplying leader expresses gratitude and acknowledges team achievements. They regularly thank team members for their efforts and provide sincere recognition privately and publicly. Celebrating successes is also vital; it boosts morale and promotes a sense of accomplishment. This leader encourages a culture where success is shared and appreciated, fostering an environment that enhances motivation, engagement, and team spirit.

3. **Leads a Mission of Just Cause.** A multiplying leader motivates their team by rallying them around a just cause beyond individual goals. They establish a clear, inspiring vision that has a positive societal impact, effectively communicating its significance and how it aligns with a more meaningful outcome. They promote ethical behavior and integrity, enabling team members to make decisions consistent with the mission's values. Such leaders empower individuals, fostering collaboration and inclusivity while valuing diverse perspectives. They constantly reinforce the importance of the just cause, adapting strategies as needed and inspiring resilience. By leading this way, they enhance performance, impact beyond immediate results, and inspire their team to work towards the greater good.

4. **Creates a Culture of Kindness.** A multiplying leader fosters a culture of kindness by modeling kindness, promoting respect and empathy, and valuing everyone's contributions. They highlight and celebrate acts of kindness and encourage supportive, respectful communication within the team. They prioritize self-care and well-being, promote work-life balance, and provide constructive, respectful feedback. By consistently practicing kindness, they foster a positive, collaborative culture that motivates everyone to contribute their best.

5. **Provides Clarity and Direction.** A multiplying leader offers clear direction by articulating the team's goals, expectations, and vision, helping members align their efforts for desired outcomes. They set clear, measurable goals and performance standards and foster a shared vision that inspires collective action. They provide guidance, encourage open communication, and are adaptive to changing circumstances, adjusting goals and directions as needed. Such leaders empower their teams by fostering a clear understanding of their roles and the mission, enabling informed decision-making and influential contributions to success.

6. **Focuses on Mentoring Others.** A multiplying leader mentors others by setting clear goals and sharing knowledge. They foster a team-wide culture of learning. They provide constructive feedback and create a supportive, trust-based environment. By encouraging autonomy, they promote innovation and ownership within the team. Through their behavior, they serve as role models while providing growth opportunities and celebrating successes to boost morale. Crucially, they nurture individual relationships, tailoring their mentoring approach to meet the unique needs of each team member. Through these practices, they cultivate a team capable of confidently operating and thriving.

7. **Equips People to Solve Problems.** A multiplying leader equips people to solve problems by fostering an environment of autonomy and creativity. They encourage team members to take ownership of challenges, providing necessary tools and training to tackle issues independently. This leader promotes open discussion, divergent thinking, and risk-taking, which helps create innovative solutions. They also help individuals develop critical thinking skills by engaging them in complex projects, asking probing questions, and challenging them to view problems from multiple perspectives. By doing so, a multiplying leader nurtures a team of capable problem solvers, ready to take on the challenges they face.

The next logical steps in multiplying leadership involve continual learning, feedback, and adjustment. Multiplying leaders should deepen their understanding of each team member's capabilities and growth needs. Regular feedback is essential, both giving and receiving, as it fosters a culture of continuous improvement and open communication. These leaders should also adjust their strategies based on the evolving needs of their team and organization. Exploring advanced leadership training and mentorship programs can provide further insights and skills to enhance their multiplying impact. Lastly, they should keep identifying opportunities to delegate responsibilities, empowering team members to develop leadership skills. This iterative process ensures the multiplying effect continues flourishing, nurturing a robust, resilient, and innovative team.

In conclusion, the journey of a multiplying leader is perpetual, filled with growth, learning, and adaptability. Their primary mission is to inspire, empower, and equip their team members to become the best versions of themselves, hence fostering a culture of shared leadership and innovation. The process might be complex and challenging, but the reward—a resilient, skilled, and self-driven team—is immeasurable. As multiplying leaders evolve and adapt to the changing needs of their team, they not only enhance the overall team performance but also cultivate a lasting legacy of leadership.

Diversify Your Skills

We live in a very fast-paced environment. Moore's Law, named after Intel's Gordon Moore, posits that the number of transistors in a circuit doubles every two years while the cost of the circuits decreases over time. The world's computing power is constantly increasing, and we need to accelerate with it. With the speed of technological change, individuals must work to keep up by continually learning and adapting to the changes in technology. Having a diversity of skills and talents will put you in a strong position. Here are some things you can do to diversify your work:

 KEY STRATEGIES

- Cultivate a culture of innovation. Serve as an example by sharing what you're studying or learning about. Apply new concepts to existing structures. Admit when you learn new lessons or when things have not gone as planned.

- Embrace emerging technologies. Move toward learning about innovations rather than running from them.

- Encourage cross-functional collaboration. Bringing other departments or organizations into your work can enhance the talents available.

- Empower a learning mindset. Trying something new is complex, and people may avoid it because they fear failure. Work to build a culture that embraces consistent learning and occasional errors (with lessons learned).

- Trust your team. It is essential to provide trust and wiggle room for the people taking on innovation and diversification. Communicating regularly and often about successes and failures is critical for continuous improvement.

The field of educational technology is always changing. Your ability to learn new things, adapt, and lead your team through change will be essential as you diversify. Know and understand your current wheelhouse. Are you an expert in a certain field? For what topics do colleagues approach you seeking advice? An inventory of your existing strengths will help you understand where you could work to diversify.

Keep an eye on world trends and always think of the future. What should we learn about right now? How will this trend impact the way you do your work? Where will you get this knowledge and expertise? Keeping track of the latest innovations, research, and trends helps you see the latest opportunities and where your current strategies must adapt to prepare for the next big thing.

Expand your knowledge and skills. With innovations come new opportunities. What interests you? You do not need to become a subject matter expert, but it is wise to know and understand the newest trends so you can acknowledge what they are and relay how those changes may impact your corner of the world.

It is one thing to know and learn new things; it is another skill to apply that new knowledge to the context of your work or life. Collaborating with others and discussing recent trends allows you to receive feedback from diverse sources. How do the changes impact them? What will they need to learn and understand before they can be successful in the new environment? When you diversify your portfolio, knowing how the latest innovations impact the parts of life you influence is essential. In the educational space, talking with colleagues, students, parents, and policymakers can all help you to diversify your expertise.

Incorporate cultural sensitivity and respect into your new skills. Looking at all innovations from the end user's point of view and receiving consistent feedback from multiple populations will ensure that your solutions work well for the populations you serve.

While you are working to diversify your knowledge and expertise, work to include others in your learning. Letting your team know what you are thinking about or studying can invite others into your learning journey. Collectively, your team could make significant headway as you all learn about a new concept and work to apply it to your current context.

Throughout your diversification journey, identify ways to measure impact. If you apply a new concept to an existing procedure, how will you collect data to know if the change is making a difference? Setting up a data collection system at the start of a project will provide valuable information as you move through the implementation stages. It can inform you whether you've met the desired target goals or show where gaps need filling before the diversified project can be called a success.

Diversifying and bringing forward change can be scary for some. There are things you can do within your team and culture to help support the rapid change that is before you. Build a culture of innovation where your team takes calculated risks and tunes into lessons learned. Provide a safe space for creativity and innovation to help break the status quo of your organization. Encourage your staff to embrace new technologies and explore new tools, platforms, or approaches that build efficiencies into your current job. As a leader, you can foster collaboration between cross-functional teams by providing the time, space, and platforms for people to apply new knowledge to an existing process.

Through this all, embracing the growth mindset and acknowledging that this is new information for all of us is essential. Setting the expectation that we may not get it right the first, second, or third time should be the norm. Helping to align the new concepts learned into existing organizational goals will help your team see that the work toward diversification is essential to serving our populations with the most innovative and well-thought-out systems and processes.

From Words to Actions
The Consistent Beat of Authentic Leadership

Think of leaders you know whose thoughts, words, and actions consistently demonstrate authenticity. We trust these leaders because they are honest. We know where we stand with them because we understand what they value. They lead with their hearts as well as their heads. They lead with a purpose that shines through in their brand. Who doesn't want to be a leader like that?

The most effective leaders have nothing to hide and nothing to prove; they know how to battle insecurity and lead with influence (Owolabi, 2020). Being authentic cannot be turned on and off. We connect with others authentically, or we don't. The connection is either real and we feel safe, or it's not and we don't.

We must dig deep and assess our leadership's actual level of authenticity. Are we openly sharing information with those in our organization? Do we genuinely care about those we lead? Do our values waver when the going gets tough?

THE ISTE STANDARDS

Chapter 7, aligned with the **Connected Learner Standard (3.5)**, explores the significance of regularly engaging in reflective practices that support personal and professional growth and well-being. This chapter helps us understand leadership authenticity at a deeper level. Authentic leaders connect with other people in a transformative way. It's tricky because, as a leader, we must deliver. At the same time, we must be empathetic and keep each other's best interests in mind. How do we balance that? We do it by achieving a work-life balance. We know what we stand for, and we build our personal and organizational brand based on authenticity. We empower others to be authentic so they feel safe and supported. We carve out dedicated time for reflection in our schedules to pause, step back from day-to-day responsibilities, and reflect on their progress and growth.

Achieve Work-Life Balance without Guilt

As Edtech Leaders, we must acknowledge that technology, especially smartphones, has made us accessible to people in our work and personal lives 24/7 (Washington, 2020). The line between work time and personal time has decidedly blurred. Successful Edtech Leaders strive to achieve a healthy work-life balance. Some refer to this balance as "managing boundaries," and others use the phrase "work-life integration." Regardless of what we call it, the ability to avoid being consumed by the vast responsibilities of today's Edtech Leader is a common goal for most, and it can be challenging to accomplish.

Achieving balance doesn't necessarily mean there is a problem with checking email for a few minutes at night to help you organize the following day. Likewise, feel guilt-free if you have a moment between meetings or projects at work to schedule a personal appointment. To achieve a work-life balance, set clear expectations for yourself and others, create time for yourself personally and professionally that is free of distractions, and set boundaries for the workday. Ellen Ernst Kossek points out the need for individuals to manage the boundaries between work and life, otherwise known as boundary management. This strategy is not only vital for you, but also for your team. Achieving a work-life balance is a form of professional development, not just for ourselves but for the benefit of those who work with us.

As an authentic Edtech Leader, strive to help your team be successful. By modeling a balanced life, you are helping them achieve balance, which is vital to their success and well-being. They take their cues from you! (Kossek 2016).

KEY STRATEGIES

- Set priorities and boundaries. Priorities involve identifying and ranking your professional and personal life's most important tasks, goals, and values. Boundaries help you protect your free time as well as your physical, mental, and emotional health.

- Set personal and professional goals. Goal setting promotes self-awareness, allowing us to prioritize our aspirations and responsibilities, and ultimately reducing stress and burnout. Moreover, achieving these goals instills a sense of accomplishment.

- Be present at work and in life. Work to foster a deeper connection to the present moment.

- Take time for yourself. Recharge your mental and physical energy, ensuring you approach work with renewed focus and creativity.

- Accept your lack of superpowers. Understanding that no one possesses superhuman abilities helps set realistic expectations for ourselves and others.

Set Priorities and Boundaries

Priorities enable you to effectively allocate your time, energy, and resources toward what truly matters. What are the priorities in your life? Be honest with yourself, and don't apologize for what is important to you. Before volunteering to take on that extra task, authentic Edtech Leaders should ask themselves several key questions: Is this going to help me fulfill my role, reach a goal, or find enjoyment? If not, then tactfully decline. Silence can be a good thing sometimes for those of us who are type A and want to be the first to raise our hand! (Lupu & Ruiz-Castro, 2021).

Boundaries define acceptable and unacceptable behavior and serve to protect your well-being and maintain your mental, emotional, and physical health. Define your workday boundaries. These boundaries may look different for everyone. Edtech Leaders do have emergencies at times. Determine what constitutes real emergencies and communicate this to your team and colleagues.

Use technology to your advantage to streamline your work and home life. Consider using scheduling tools to manage your time or online shopping services to save time on errands. Avoid emailing your team or colleagues during non-working hours and weekends to respect their free time if at all possible. If you choose to respond to emails after work or on weekends, schedule delivery during regular working hours. Real emergencies merit a phone call or text. Clearly communicate that other issues should be entered as a work order or service ticket. These ideas help you to manage boundaries and be in control of your timetable. Don't hesitate to let others know that you generally do not answer emails at night, and don't apologize or feel the need to explain.

An authentic Edtech Leader focuses on helping their team succeed! What better way to help them succeed and grow than to model a healthy work–home balance?

GUILT-FREE BALANCE

My schedule generally meant leaving work by 5:00 p.m. Monday to Thursday; Fridays, I left earlier. To accommodate those rare times I needed to leave work early for family events, I might work a few nights a week after my children went to bed. Sometimes, I had my laptop in the room when the children were doing homework or watching TV in the den. Generally, this work revolved around reading articles or researching a problem.

Note I didn't say every night! I did not work on weekends. I checked my email on Sunday nights while watching TV to make for a better Monday. Sanity was a part of my balance! Was I right or wrong? There is no correct answer. Find your guilt-free balance.

—DONNA WILLIAMSON

Set Personal and Professional Goals

Keep a current list of your personal and professional goals. Understand the big-picture district goals and collaboratively establish goals for your team. Write them down and keep them within sight. This list can help you refocus when you are in the weeds and feel overwhelmed. Revisit, modify, add, or eliminate personal and professional goals when needed. Some goals may change over time.

Divide your tasks and put them into "buckets." These buckets should be aligned with your goals. By dividing the tasks from one continuous list into lists with related tasks tied to specific goals, you can focus on one bucket at a time. Assign tentative dates to the tasks so that you can see that not everything needs your attention today.

Be patient and persistent in achieving work and personal goals. Prioritize self-care goals and the things that matter most to you. Life, as you know, is a journey, not a sprint.

Be Present at Work and in Life

Being present at work and in life enhances interpersonal relationships by showing authentic interest and active listening.

Set aside time outside work to be genuinely present with your family and friends. Both at work and at home, eliminate distractions. The best way to eliminate distractions is to be prepared and organized. It is hard to be present if you are constantly concerned that you will drop one of the many balls you juggle in the air.

Let your family and close friends know the best times to reach you during the day and when you have meetings or events that make you unavailable. Discuss the best ways to contact you—text, phone, or email. Provide family and friends with a strategy for reaching you in case of an emergency.

Professionally, clarify with your team and peers what is considered an emergency and how to handle those emergencies. In edtech, there are always events that others feel are an emergency. Robust, well-thought-out processes can eliminate much of this stress.

Keep a good calendar for both personal and professional items. Make sure you can see the complete picture of your professional and personal life simultaneously. This tactic helps avoid double booking. Keep open times to allow for the unexpected.

Learn to manage email. Set up folders so that the highest priority emails go to folders that you check regularly. Consider numbering the folders or labels so that they are listed in priority order. Communicate the expectations for an emergency service ticket. A fire in the wiring closet should not be an email!

These ideas can eliminate many of the distractions that prevent us from being present at work and at home. Planning and organization go a long way toward making us feel that we are in charge of our lives.

There Are No Superpowers

Recognizing limitations fosters teamwork in both work and home environments. By understanding that none of us have superpowers, we can better appreciate the skills and strengths of others, leading to more effective collaboration and synergy within teams and in our personal lives.

We can't state too often that successful Edtech Leaders are authentic with themselves and others. You can't always be great at everything. List the priorities for the week. When asked to do something else, refer to the list. If it is not on the list, refrain from jumping to commit. Sometimes, the unexpected becomes a priority. In that case, look at the list to see what you can move to the following week. Organization and planning lead to peace of mind. Don't hesitate to ask for help.

In your professional life, determine your support team. This support team may include people in your department, other individuals in the district, or outsourced vendors. Delegate to your support team when possible. Remember that they can only meet expectations if you clearly state them, and they can only succeed if you provide them with the knowledge and tools to do so.

Before moving into an Edtech Leadership role, you must have candid conversations with the most important people in your personal life about the anticipated time commitment required to succeed in the role. There might need to be a shift in current roles in your personal life. Build a support team. It may be family members, neighbors, or friends. Consider asking for help with things like carpooling to after-school activities or feeding pets.

You may need to outsource some tasks both at work and at home. No matter how hard you work, how many hours you commit, how organized you are, or how capable you are, there are often simply not enough hours in the day. Again, go back to your priorities.

How will you balance your work with your personal life? Are you a separator, striving for a greater divide between work and personal life? Or are you an integrator who prefers to blend work and nonwork roles, often choosing to work during vacations, or have you selected a career that overlaps with your interest in edtech as a hobby (Kossek 2016)?

Build a Brand for Yourself

Do you have a brand? Do you know what you value and what inspires you? Is it evident to the people who know you? How about the people who don't know you? Having a brand is essential as you establish yourself as a leader. Your branding shows through in your confidence, attitude, and interactions with people. Your brand may not fit with societal norms, and that's okay. You are an original.

 ## KEY STRATEGIES

- Develop a personal mission statement on which to base your brand. Your mission statement will ensure consistency and focus your branding efforts.

- Identify what you want to deliver to your audience and stick with it. Know that you cannot be everything to everybody.

- If branding seems overwhelming, start small. Find one thing you want to share about your brand and start there.

- Identify the personal and professional images you want to emulate and build your brand around those things.

- Identify unique things about you and include them in your brand. Make sure your brand genuinely matches who you are.

Exactly what is your brand? Your brand is how others perceive you. As entrepreneur Gary Vaynerchuk noted in an article about personal branding, "Your personal brand is your reputation. And your reputation in perpetuity is the foundation of your career" (Vaynerchuk, 2021).

Your brand shows what you value! When creating your brand, consider what is most important to you (Rice, 2021). Who is your brand's audience? What are their needs? Do they want knowledge? Affirmation? To laugh with you? Or to think differently because of your influence? What do you want to accomplish with your brand? What do you value? How can you consistently show those values through the content you put into the world? Do you feel strongly about specific topics and support different causes or organizations?

Do you have an area of expertise? If so, what can you do to establish yourself as an expert in the field? Do you have outside interests? Sharing with the world the time you spent on your hobby also portrays what you enjoy doing and shows that you devote time to self-care.

Keep equity in mind when you are thinking about your brand. Are you causing harm or offense via anything in your posts? Are you showing authentic content that promotes respect toward others and works to elevate others from underrepresented populations? Do you exhibit and model ethical and legal use of technology?

Don't let too much time elapse between your social media interactions. We know that the absence of information allows others to make up information about you. Consistently providing content via your favorite social media helps remind the world you're still there.

Nobody likes a bragger. Make sure you approach each post with humility. How might you lift someone else up through your posts? Someone working on the same goal or with similar expertise in a subject area could benefit from your endorsement and gain followers from your professional social media community. What would your kind words about somebody else show to the world? It most likely would be viewed as unselfish and show that you are interested in elevating others.

AN AUTHENTIC BRAND

Diane Doersch's brand evolved over the years as she moved into educational technology leadership. With four daughters, she had been a Facebook user to inform her parents of family activities. As she became more involved in educational technology, she went where professionals went on social media: Twitter and LinkedIn. Those platforms allowed her to learn from her peers, curate content, and share relevant resources and information. They served as great collaborative tools where she could build her professional learning network. As she grew professionally and collaboratively in her community, she started showing colleagues her non-work life, including posts about leisure activities, such as catch-and-release fishing trips, with headlines encouraging colleagues to find a balance between work and life. While many had seen her in professional attire speaking at events like those with the Women in Technology organization in Wisconsin, it was a great contrast to see her on her fishing kayak holding a big bass or in a field driving a tractor. Through her social media posts, her colleagues could see the authentic Diane in her professional and personal activities and the causes she supports. She had successfully incorporated non-work interests into her brand.

Don't insult or offend your audience. In this politically charged environment, someone could easily be interpreted as being on one side or the other. While it is okay to have your opinions, disrespecting, cutting down, and calling names is an excellent way to lose followers. Always be aware of your audience and the content they will tolerate.

People like to engage with leaders who are interested in them. Do your interactions result in you talking about yourself, or do you engage others and show interest in the person you're talking with? Asking about what makes a person tick is a beautiful way to learn more about people and an opportunity to expand your knowledge.

If you want your brand to exude collaboration, inclusivity, joy, and teamwork, consider how you may show these characteristics when interacting with people. Find ways to let your discussion partner know you are hearing them. Body language is essential in offering warmth and approachability. Maintaining eye contact during a conversation, leaning in, tilting your head, or nodding when the other person is speaking to you are ways to show that you are listening and are interested.

Personal branding can take on other forms. Electronic signatures, logos, and websites should all exude your brand. The possibilities of branding yourself are endless, and new methods pop up in the most unexpected ways. Remember that as a leadership figure, people are watching you. What do you consistently want them to see?

Create the Organization's Brand

Thriving Edtech Leaders create a brand for their organization or team. Think of your organization's brand as the messaging and overall experience that distinguishes your organization from others.

The organization's brand should shape the overall perception of your organization's capabilities and services. What do your customers and stakeholders think about when they hear the organization's name? An authentic organizational brand helps to build recognition, trust, and loyalty.

KEY STRATEGIES

- Make an emotional connection. Use emotion to stir up feelings of commitment to the brand.

- Solicit feedback. Align organization feedback with the brand message. For example, if your organization's brand is *student learning first*, seek input by asking, Do you feel our organization cares about student learning first, over and above everything else?

- Place the brand logo and statement on posters, shirts, cups, or anything you can think of. Be consistent across all platforms and communications.

- Leverage storytelling. Find authentic stories that capture your organization's brand. Use variations of a consistent storyline in all communications.

- Create a brand message script. Some staff members need a blueprint to follow during conversations. A script will provide consistent messaging.

Make an Emotional Connection

The brand message should weave a tapestry of emotions. Ask yourself what you want folks to feel when they encounter anyone from the organization.

Solicit Feedback

Feedback is the compass guiding you toward building a distinguished brand message. First, make it easy for people to provide feedback. Ease of use is critical, whether through conversations in meetings, surveys, social media polls, or a dedicated feedback form on a website.

Building the organization's brand starts with questions that stir up the kinds of feelings that we want others to experience:

- What is the organization's promise?

- How will the organization demonstrate that promise?

- How does the organization's commitment align with its vision, purpose, and values?

- How will we create an expectation of reliability to deliver on our promise?

- How will we use our voice, tone, and personal manners to communicate with our customers?

Next Steps

Now that we have a draft brand message, CEO and best-selling author Donald Miller suggests that we analyze the brand message carefully. "Can you say it easily? Is it simple, relevant, and repeatable? Can your entire team repeat your organization's brand message in a compelling way?" (2017). Being able to clarify the message so the organization understands the brand and can communicate it effectively is crucial.

Create a brand identity. Gather information from the first two strategies, including emotions and feedback. Fold in the organizational visionary planning document. Continue to drill down to the details and fine-tune your brand identity. Who does your organization support? Is it students, educators, or a board of trustees? What are their goals? What creates their success? Mold your message to mirror their needs.

Use your imagination. Make your brand one that resonates in the mind of your organization and with those you serve, such your students, teachers, and administrators.

LEAD THE WAY

During my tenure as the Chief Technology Officer for a mega-large school district serving over a hundred thousand students, the school district's brand was "LEAD the Way." The acronym *LEAD* stood for *Learn, Empower, Aspire,* and *Dream.* I aligned the school district's brand with my organization's brand, which was "LEADing World-Class Technology and Information Systems." Once I created this organizational brand for my team, we strove to be world-class. I have extensive knowledge of Total Quality Management (TQM) systems and served as a National Institute for Standards and Technology (NIST) Baldrige Performance Excellence Program examiner (nist.gov/baldrige). I used my TQM knowledge and skills to brand my organization, aligned with NIST and performance excellence. How do we align words with actions? With every service activity and leadership activity, we ask ourselves, are we world-class? Are we providing world-class services? Are we leading the way? We set all performance expectations towards leadership in world-class service and technology, which became our team's unique image. It was effective and influential!

—FRANKIE JACKSON

Following are some sample brand messages to inspire you:

- *Supporting student success by improving teaching and learning*
- *Amazing technology for every student*
- *Leading with superior world-class technology service*
- *Inspiring great achievement*
- *Finding ways to engage and delight our students*
- *Your success is our success.*
- *Creating WOW in every technology touch point*
- *Delighting our customers*
- *Student learning first*
- *Visionary planning focused on transforming learning with technology*
- *Student success!*

Create a brand logo. Make it colorful, attractive, and multimedia-rich. You can use it in all channels of communication. The logo must remind you who you serve and what you stand for.

Here is the fun part. Once you have developed the brand message and logo, use it! Be creative. Place the brand logo on posters, shirts, cups, and any other swag. Remember your websites, social media, and packaging? Brand logos can also adorn digital devices and cases.

Leverage Storytelling

Storytelling is the secret sauce that adds flavor and depth to your brand. Author Chase Barlow (2020) recommends finding stories that will significantly impact emotions. Consider using authentic stories about overcoming a specific challenge and tie that to the organization's vision and values. Tell a story about a student using a take-home device, which increased his academic performance by thirty percent!

Be sure to infuse your storytelling with relatable emotions to create a connection, whether it's joy, inspiration, or empathy. As an Edtech Leader, we can think of many stories that speak to the value of technology and its impact on our students.

Feature real people and students. Highlight authentic stories of individuals connected to your brand, because authenticity is magnetic. Share a struggle, such as the third grader who was struggling to read and couldn't access technology resources.

As you think about your story, it's not just about the words; it's about the emotions, the characters, and the journey. When done right, storytelling creates a brand people believe in and buy into.

Create a Brand Message Script

Writing a brand message script will help you encapsulate a powerful brand message. Once you develop a written script that outlines the dialogue, actions, and instructions that support your organization's brand message, you can use it repeatedly for many purposes. The script is handy when you are working to pass the brand communication along to your team. Plan to model using the brand in your communications, especially to those you serve. Your team will likely pick up on this strategy and use it themselves.

Some staff members will appreciate a blueprint to follow during conversations with those they serve. A script will provide consistent storytelling and a powerful framework for spreading your brand. Following are some sample scripts:

Identify the core brand message you want to express. "What sets our organization apart is _____. I'm excited to share our brand. It is _____."

Grab the attention of the person you are speaking to in the opening. Use a bold statement, a thought-providing question, or a captivating story. "Here's an example of how we impact student learning. We _____."

Emphasize the vision and values that define your brand. For example, if your values are innovative, student-focused, and trusted, stir up emotions around those values and the organization's vision. "One of our values is _____. *or* Our vision is to _____. Let me tell you a great story about _____."

Address a pain point. If you know that teachers need more student devices, acknowledge the challenges, and show empathy for the situation. Talk about how your brand provides solutions. "Our strategic plan includes _____ which is going to help solve your specific need. Let me tell you how." Describe how and when the solution will be available.

Include a testimonial or success story. Talk about a real-life example of others who are benefiting from your brand. Authentic testimonials add credibility and relatability. "Let me tell you about how _____ is serving _____ well."

Add individuality. The script can match the communicator's personality, whether quirky or humorous. That's okay. The character of your staff adds uniqueness and sincerity. Let their personality shine through.

Practice the script with your team. Make sure everyone in the organization is generally consistent. Ensure the delivery aligns with the intended message, tone, and emotion. Have fun with it!

The brand message script is a living document. As your brand message evolves, so too should your script. Regularly revisit and refine it to ensure it continues to communicate your brand's story and values effectively.

Jump Aboard the Allyship

What exactly is *allyship*? Allyship has a powerful impact on the workplace. According to the Center for Creative Leadership, "Allyship in the workplace refers to actions, behaviors, and practices that leaders take to support, amplify, and advocate with others, most especially with individuals who don't belong to the same social identities as themselves" (Dias & Hamill, 2023).

As an Edtech Leader, you have a unique opportunity to develop, leverage, optimize, build, and coach allies. And as an evolving leader, you have a distinct opportunity to create positive change one day at a time by advancing other leaders in an organization. Allies can exert powerful leverage and create and support a workplace culture that allows people to be empowered to be their authentic selves.

 KEY STRATEGIES

- Use your allies. Use your allies as a sounding board to promote your ideas.

- Look for allies. When looking for allies, don't limit yourself to your current network. Revisit your old contacts.

- Develop a relationship. In the early stages of developing a relationship with an ally, focus on understanding them rather than asking for favors. Look for ways to mutually benefit each other.

- Define expectations. Define your expectations for being an ally and strive to meet them. Your success should not be isolated; aim to contribute to the success of others in their respective areas.

- Relationships begin with basic trust. Can you count on each other to do tasks correctly and on time? As your allyship deepens, you should be able to warn each other of potential problems and provide help.

Allies can be compelling catalysts for change and create a much more level playing field for minorities and women in an organization. Properly leveraged, an ally can be a resource to help leaders, established and emerging, build new communication strategies free from judgment and risk. This is conducive to being your authentic self, speaking openly, being vulnerable, and supporting each other. Leveraging your allies builds your natural drive to speak for yourself *and* for others.

In any organization, this leverage begins with leadership, and leadership is the starting point for influence. Employees often look to their leaders for guidance on the organization's priorities and dynamics. Embracing diverse thoughts and genuine viewpoints offers a chance for diverse voices to be recognized. Making well-informed decisions can reduce errors, present new opportunities, and help you acquire influence and allies you don't currently have. By making informed choices, you can attain significant influence, open new pathways, explore fresh possibilities, reduce major errors, and enhance understanding (Paul & Elder, 2014).

One issue with allyship involves the ability to differentiate between building versus leveraging relationships. Women leaders are often more likely to struggle with this differentiation. Sheryl Abshire clearly felt this when she became one of the first female principals in her school district. She quickly realized she needed to make friends and win over enemies. She knew that women tend to be fantastic relationship builders, but they are inclined to be less adept at leveraging relationships. They're more than willing to dedicate their time and effort to understanding others, providing assistance, empathizing with issues, offering guidance, and fostering close relationships. However, the idea of interacting with allies in a manner that advances their own ambitions is more difficult.

Abshire knew from watching other women in the field that sometimes, women in a new position focus on learning everything and making sure they can do the work well before they start interacting purposefully. They want to feel fully ready before they start making connections. But she observed that men who begin new jobs usually think, 'Who do I need to know to do well here?' They often believe success comes from who you know, not what or how you do. No matter the gender, leaders in a new position will benefit from both building *and* leveraging allyships.

Who Are Your Allies?

Allies are friends, bosses, supporters, team members, and any others who want you to do well. They understand your goals, believe they're important, feel involved, and do what they can to help you succeed. They help you find what you need to do challenging tasks. They tell others about your excellent work. Allies are crucial for a promising career; leveraging them is essential to success. CEO and co-founder of AngelList Naval Ravikant tells us that "in an age of infinite leverage, judgment is the most important skill" (Fromet, 2023). Being able to ascertain who will be the most supportive and effective in helping you to succeed and advance your career is a critical judgment skill.

Advantages in work and life can be due to many things—such as your sex, gender, race, age, social class, physical ability, mental condition, education, or whether you're a citizen. Just because you have an advantage in one area doesn't mean you have it in every area. But wherever you do have an advantage, you can use it to help those who don't, becoming an ally. You might later leverage that allyship.

In Abshire's career of more than thirty years as an Edtech Leader, she recognized the power of being an ally. She found it could be as simple as encouraging new employees who were nervous to share their thoughts. Sometimes, it's noticing the person who doesn't talk much and giving them a chance to speak.

Allyship is not an entirely altruistic act. Being a supportive friend isn't just about helping others. Being an ally can help someone become their best self and improve your team's overall results. A workplace culture that values and leverages allyship, supportive friendships, inclusion, and diversity can lead to incredible new ideas and profound innovation.

Turning Enemies into Allies

How can you turn your enemies into allies? How can you transform what might seem like a negative relationship into a win-win? Have you ever had a bad relationship at work that brought you and your team down? It's relatively common for this to happen, especially in a competitive leadership environment. Workplace conflicts are common and can hurt an organization by draining energy and halting progress. According to Uzzi and Dunlap in the *Harvard Business Review*, the 3R Method can transform conflicts into positive relationships and therefore build allyship (Uzzi & Dunlap, 2012). Here's how the 3R Method works:

1. First, use *redirection* to steer your rival's negative feelings away from the conflict (take the rival to lunch, find something you have in common).

2. This prepares the way for step two, *reciprocity*, to build a relationship. The key here is to give before asking—provide something valuable to the rival to encourage future cooperation.

3. The final step is *rationality*, where you clarify what you expect from the new relationship. This ensures your efforts don't seem insincere. It encourages the rival to see the benefits of working together.

The 3Rs can help fix a rivalry and create new allies. Allies are not just beneficial but vital for a thriving career. They don't merely contribute to your success; they amplify it.

Driving the Future of Learning
The Role of Competence, Collaboration, and Change Agents

Over the past four decades, the landscape of education has been reshaped by technology. Technology is no longer a "nice to have"; technology has become integral to every facet of the learning ecosystem. Today's Edtech Leaders wear multiple hats, managing technology integration across departments and stakeholders, including students, teachers, administrators, parents, and the wider community. In this environment, success hinges on more than technical expertise—it demands exceptional leadership.

Savvy Edtech Leaders recognize that their role extends beyond their technical knowledge. Managing *things* is the easy part of the job; it's the leadership of *people* that can be challenging. You must possess the skills to rally support and commitment from stakeholders, a trait indispensable for driving initiatives forward.

A valuable skill is the ability to translate complex technical issues, processes, or solutions into understandable statements for lay stakeholders while adeptly engaging in detailed technical discussions with your technical staff and vendor partners. As a change agent, Edtech Leaders must be able to communicate to all stakeholders that technology not only allows them to do things better but to do better things (Gura, 2018).

THE ISTE STANDARDS

Chapter 8 connects to several ISTE Education Leader Standards: **Visionary Planner (3.2)**, **Empowering Leader (3.3)**, and **Systems Designer (3.4)**.

Standard 3.2, which focuses on engaging others in establishing a vision and strategic plan for transforming learning with technology, is particularly relevant to your role as an Edtech Leader. Chapter 8 highlights the importance of cultivating a shared vision that aligns with the organization's core beliefs and goals, emphasizing your crucial role in shaping conversations and objectives to meet the learning ecosystem's needs and aspirations.

Standard 3.3 emphasizes empowering educators to use technology innovatively to enrich teaching and learning. This chapter outlines the leadership skills needed to rally support and commitment from stakeholders and the importance of continuously honing strengths, talents, and skills to distinguish oneself in Edtech Leadership.

Standard 3.4—which focuses on building teams and systems to implement, sustain, and continually improve the use of technology to support learning—is a cornerstone of effective Edtech Leadership. The content in this chapter emphasizes the profound impact you can have on the learning ecosystem by translating complex technical issues into understandable statements for stakeholders, communicating effectively with all parties involved, and possessing the foresight to address concerns before they arise, guiding learning organizations toward a future where technology and learning intertwine seamlessly.

Improve Morale and Boost Productivity

There are numerous philosophies to choose from when discussing an organization's culture. In the context of this section, the culture is the shared mission and goals of the organization in conjunction with an established set of core values, beliefs, and acceptable behaviors. A positive culture is one where the entire learning community feels cared for, included, and valued. As the Edtech Leader in an organization, you can influence the culture within the technology department as well as the organization's overall culture. When students feel valued, they are more engaged. When the school administration, teachers, and staff trust each other and the organization's leaders, they are more candid and willing to share their ideas and perspectives. They are more comfortable making decisions and leading if their voices are heard. When parents feel valued and that their students are safe and intellectually engaged, they have confidence in the school environment and often take a more active and positive role in the process.

In a healthy culture, everyone is actively interested in and supportive of student achievement and positive behaviors. Attendance goes up for staff and students, and parental distrust goes down. An organization's culture affects the recruitment and retention of teachers, administrative leaders, and support staff. Likewise, the technology department's culture affects the recruitment and retention of its members. A healthy culture doesn't just happen in a school district, organization, or department; it requires intentional effort and nurturing.

 KEY STRATEGIES

- Research, watch, and listen to learn about an organization's culture. We cannot stress enough the value of knowing an organization's mission, goals, core values, and behaviors.

- Make promoting a positive culture within your team or department a priority.

- Be prepared to reevaluate your initial perceptions of an organization or department's culture as you observe, listen, and learn.

Learn about an Organization's Culture

Research the organization. Read articles about what the organization promotes and how it recognizes achievement. Watch employees' body language. Compare your observations with the organization's website content, personnel manual, and what's said during the interview or onboarding process. Carve out time to visit the buildings served. Is the administrative staff always behind closed doors? Are they ever in the halls, greeting students and staff? Do you get a feel for what is valued?

After observing for a while, look successful leaders in the organization you model the type of leadership style you aspire to. Ask questions that will provide insight into how things *really* work. Sample questions may include asking about the process for continued growth, the best venue to express feedback, and how to collaborate with other departments. Ask about norms and practices that are core to being a school community member. Ask teachers casual questions about their school, what they teach, etc. The main goal is to get them talking, then truly listen to what is said and note what is not said. As you ask questions to apply the appropriate lens, you may want to begin with, "How long have you been in the district?"

Look for patterns. What is consistent across all people you talk to? What is important to the organization? These patterns can help you understand the culture.

Promote a Positive Culture

A new employee can enhance a team's culture or tank it. A cultural fit does not mean that the person is just like you or others in the department, but rather that they share core values and overarching goals. As you create a diverse and inclusive team, new hires who appreciate the culture you are trying to create in your department will have greater job satisfaction, productivity, and teamwork success. Employees have a higher retention rate when they understand and value the department's culture. You can teach someone skills; you can't teach them to like the way things are done in the district or within your department. Encourage new hires to ask questions through every phase leading up to hiring and after.

Let's look at several tactics that provide a new hire a closer look at the district and department culture. During the interview, discuss the organization's culture, including its mission, goals, core values, and behaviors; during the onboarding process, include a focus on culture, soft skills, and the organizational structure. Emphasize the importance of diversity and inclusion, equity, empathy, punctuality, collaboration, and not only tolerance but encouragement of differing ideas and points of view.

Once onboard, assign the new hire a coworker who understands and values the culture to serve as a thought partner. Provide an opportunity for new hires to ask questions and give feedback.

Create an environment for capacity building and growth. This starts with building trust and relationships. Most importantly, do what you say you will do. Honor confidentiality, and always have your team members' backs. Don't throw team members under the bus when things get difficult! Give constructive feedback on problem areas privately.

Listen and value the ideas of your team. Be open to feedback. Encourage staff members to share their ideas and suggestions and be open to change. Not only will the feedback help you to identify areas where the department can improve, but it will also let the team know their input is valued. Create a collaborative environment. Encourage staff members to work together and share ideas. Collaboration creates a sense of community and fosters innovation.

Sometimes, things go differently than planned; be flexible and prepared to make changes as needed. When changes are necessary or the unexpected happens, be positive. A positive attitude is contagious. Communicate clearly. If you are still determining the actions needed, either wait to discuss it or let your team know you are still working through logistics. Vagueness leads to uncertainty and misunderstanding.

Discuss and support establishing a work-life balance, and respect employees' time away from work whenever possible. Model self-care. Encourage team members to take their vacation time and to rest and relax.

Recognize and reward staff members for their accomplishments, and celebrate successes including milestones along the way. When staff members do a good job, be sure to let them know. Positive reinforcement boosts morale and creates a positive work environment. When the department achieves a goal, take some time to celebrate. Doing so creates a sense of accomplishment and builds team spirit.

Build a New Toolkit

When you assume an edtech leadership role after already working within an organization, your outlook may undergo a transformation, influencing both the nature of your discussions and the purpose behind your tasks. How you navigate these adjustments is pivotal in shaping the kind of leader you will ultimately become.

To succeed, an Edtech Leader must anticipate and adapt to shifts in mindset, relationships, and types of work that come with becoming the Edtech Leader of an organization. The dynamics with your colleagues and the scope of your responsibilities may change. You will now be entrusted with and held accountable for a more substantial pool of resources and critical services. Your goals must align with the organization's goals and work to support the organization's strategic plan. How do we cultivate these authentic Edtech Leadership skills?

 KEY STRATEGIES

- Recognize the characteristics of authentic and effective Edtech Leadership. Reflect on your leadership traits and look for growth opportunities.

- Adopt a growth mindset in how you handle people and work responsibilities, contributions to the organization, and your alignment with the district's vision and goals. Be adaptable.

- Build a leadership toolkit that includes honing your soft skills. Continue to add to your leadership toolkit throughout your career.

Characteristics of Great Edtech Leadership

Successful Edtech Leaders encapsulate the qualities of effective and authentic leadership. They continuously evaluate their leadership style and are open to strategies that help them grow. Take a moment to ponder your current traits using the list and descriptions below. Identify areas that may warrant concentrated attention.

Add value. You fill shoes that the organization determined you were right for! Why do you think the organization hired you? What qualities did the selection committee see in you? Identify and exceed expectations.

Exercise strong team-building skills. Seek to build a highly functional, balanced, cross-trained, diverse, and inclusive team. List the skill sets needed within the team and cross-reference the list with team members' skill sets. Find the gaps and provide opportunities for training, determine outsourcing opportunities, or make the case for additional staff. Model inclusivity in language and actions.

Handle conflict. Adopt the motto of respect before popularity. Listen to all sides before responding. Allow people to maintain their dignity. Be consistent.

Establish work norms within the department and establish transparent processes and procedures.

Build resilience. Facing and overcoming adversity builds resilience. Don't hide from it. Don't be afraid to FAIL (First Attempt In Learning).

Lead to succeed. You must lead people to succeed, not manage them. They respond positively to leaders who are ethical and fair. People need to feel trusted and that they matter. They need recognition for their efforts. Manage things; lead people.

Invest in seeing others succeed. Your job is often to teach—not always to do. Authentic Edtech Leaders accept the responsibility of investing a part of themselves in other people's success. You should not be competing with your people for recognition and credit.

Make data-influenced decisions. Act with the confidence that comes from being prepared and understanding the problem or situation. Respond in a timely manner, even if it means saying that the situation needs further review. Ask for input from the team and other departments if applicable. Build consensus among team members and other stakeholders. Avoid letting the perfect plan be the enemy of action. There will inevitably be some unknowns. Waiting for one hundred percent confidence in a decision before acting can be paralyzing.

Demonstrate accountability. You are accountable for everything your team does. Likewise, hold each individual responsible for what they need to deliver. Provide clear expectations and do status checks along the way.

Hear what people say. Listen to the words spoken but also understand the underlying ideas, concerns, and aspirations. Value diverse viewpoints and seek to foster an environment where insights from various people and departments are integrated for informed decision-making and innovative solutions.

Be visible. You will only reach a critical mass of engagement if you are as visible as your schedule allows. Schedule a time each week to visit a different department, building, or school.

Communicate concisely and regularly. Communications should come directly from the mouths of the leadership team, early and often. Effective Edtech Leaders ensure that information on the organization's website and social media sites is kept current. They help write the narrative by sharing successes. They communicate systematically and often with their team.

Adopt a Growth Mindset

To be successful in an Edtech Leadership role requires the ability to adapt. This adaptation may require a change in focus and mindset, coupled with a dedicated willingness to embrace proven leadership practices. What practices should be considered?

Relationships. A relationship reset may be necessary if you now lead the team you once were part of. Effective leadership demands that you be fair and impartial. To have favorites will cause jealousy and reduce motivation. The smaller the department, the more difficult it is not to gravitate toward people who have similar interests. Not everyone may like you, but they will respect you if you are fair and equitable.

People responsibilities. Before your leadership role, even though you were a team player, you were only responsible for your own behavior and actions. You are now responsible for the physical and mental well-being of everyone on the team and their work performance. Give frequent and clear feedback and direction.

Resource responsibilities. Remember, you manage things, but you lead people. Don't confuse the two.

Contributions. Becoming part of the organization's leadership team gives you a voice, an opportunity, and an obligation. You're accountable for your team's results and for contributing to the decisions and actions of the leadership team. Seek to contribute to the organization's overall work.

Alignment. As a team member, you may have criticized the decisions made above you. As the organization's Edtech Leader, you shouldn't. You should support the goals and objectives of the superintendent and executive team. If you cannot do this, perhaps you should make a career change. Support doesn't mean you can never ask how or why. Sometimes, you may not totally agree or see the bigger picture. The longer you are a part of the administrative team or cabinet and the more trusted and experienced you become in your role, the more you will see opportunities to offer constructive suggestions while still supporting the vision, mission, and goals.

Supplementary Skills

Emerging and veteran Edtech Leaders should endeavor to incorporate supplementary skills into their leadership toolkit. Many of these leaders previously occupied diverse leadership positions before assuming their current roles. What do successful authentic leaders have in their leadership toolbox?

- Understanding of culture
- Can-do mentality
- Great decision-making skills
- Ability to deliver value
- Ability to work at the right level
- Accountability
- Skills for handling conflict
- Confidence
- Soft skills

As you settle in, it is imperative that you start to understand the culture of the organization, the community, and, at times, individual schools or groups of schools. Take time to sit down and meet with the other leaders in the district. Walk through schools and observe.

You must also understand your department's culture to be an effective team leader. You may be following a leader who could have been more effective, and the organization hired or promoted you to make drastic changes. On the other hand, you may be following a legend. Tread with intentionality.

Acknowledge the legacy. It can be tempting for new Edtech Leaders to want to change everything in the department. You might be tempted to ignore the past and forge ahead, especially if you believe things to be a disaster. Take a moment to develop some situational awareness. Some existing team members were likely instrumental in implementing what is currently there. Choose your words carefully. Use phrases like "You've accomplished much over the past few years. I have a few ideas on how we can build on that." Or "I know I am filling some big shoes; I hope you will help me carry the plan forward."

Ease tensions. There is a good chance you are already under a microscope. Regardless of the nods of agreement you receive during each department meeting, they may look at each other with doubt once you leave the room. They are still determining how they will fit into your vision. For some of them, the environment that you are walking into is the only one they have ever known. Fear is the hardest fire you will ever have to put out. Push back agendas for a little while. Spend time talking with individuals. Discuss some of your ideas, determine who is less reluctant to change, and recruit them as champions of those changes. Clear up any misconceptions team members have as soon as possible.

Define your values and vision. Paint a picture of success. Communicate clearly and effectively. Team members will want to know what you expect and how you will change things. Take the time to explain the *why*. Control the narrative! You can grab the torch without changing the entire playbook. Use different mediums for accentuating and clarifying the vision over time. Be patient. Sometimes you have to say it like you have never said it before.

Avoid surprises. Once things settle down and you are ready to move forward, do your best to avoid surprises. Use a combination of approachability and transparency. Communicate all significant decisions, initiatives, plans, timelines, etc., internally before publicly. There will be some agendas that, due to their nature, you will not be able to share with your team until a public announcement has been made. Be quick to reassure your team in this case.

An essential objective of an Edtech Leader should be to deliver value for their organization. Value comes in many forms, such as streamlining operations, making the environment more inclusive, providing data that assists others in making sound decisions, providing equity for all stakeholders, reducing cost for services, and improving support for all users. It is crucial to identify and communicate what value means in *your* context. Set your goals, monitor progress, then tell the story, giving credit to all those who played a part.

Every action taken or decision made can cause conflict. Authentic Edtech Leaders handle conflict comfortably. They negotiate effectively, do not procrastinate on decisions that may be unpopular, and bring out the best in their people. Adopting the mantra of *respect before popularity* is a crucial building block for leadership performance.

We all face challenges in our roles. Promote a "culture of can." Nothing is permanent. Develop your skill set to weather the storms that bring adversity. Capitalize on the positives. Your positive attitude is critical if you want to keep your team positive. Strive to be the department of "Know," not the department of "No."

The organization pays its Edtech Leader to lead people that work at various levels; the job is to envision, lead, and teach—not always do. In other words, try to avoid getting in the weeds. If you're busy doing all of the work, you're probably not leading. It is critical that you adopt a mindset separate from that of an individual department member. Your job is to ensure that all members of your department are successful.

The range and complexity of factors you must consider increase significantly as the Edtech Leader. You may face significant uncertainty when you're responsible for *outlining* the path to success instead of just *following* it. When you invest time in preparing for a meeting, presentation, or difficult conversation, you speak more authoritatively and act more confidently. Your preparation may involve collaborating with peers, doing research, reviewing data, or outlining what you will say. As the leader, the department members should have confidence in you and clarity on what they need to do to be successful. They will look to you for assurance, stability, and purpose. Being a member of the leadership team also requires confidence. To prepare, clearly understand the district's long-term goals and how your team's individual work contributes to those goals, and communicate those contributions.

When accountability is shared or unclear, gaps and overlaps inevitably emerge. That's why single-point accountability is the key to successful execution. It creates an entirely different culture than the all-care-no-responsibility approach, wherein a leader diffuses accountabilities across multiple department members. One of the best tips for an authentic Edtech Leader is to be accountable for everything your department does and hold each individual responsible for what they need to deliver as part of a project.

Edtech Leaders often over-emphasize their technical or instructional skills and put soft skills on the back burner. Don't make this mistake. Soft skills include communication skills, teamwork skills, problem-solving skills, critical-thinking skills, and time-management skills.

To cultivate effective leadership, practice authentic leadership. Focus on being transparent and ethical, and sharing the information needed to make decisions while accepting others' ideas and feedback. Be willing to learn, grow, and adapt.

Be a World-Class Change Agent

Edtech Leaders have a combination of strengths, talents, and skills that set them apart from others. Sometimes you see a great leader in action and can quickly identify the factors that make them so remarkable. Perhaps they are great storytellers who can convey ideas and inspiration through their oratorial musings. They may be a subject matter expert. The leader may be a gifted connector who can see which people can best work together to achieve the desired outcome. Charisma may ooze from the leader in their warmth, smile, genuineness, and body language. They ask questions about you or your project, are authentically interested in what you do, wholeheartedly support your cause, and will do what they can to help you succeed.

 KEY STRATEGIES

- Never underestimate your influence on others. No matter where you are on the organizational chart, how you treat people, talk about people when they're not in the room, and support others is noticed.

- When the people you support do something that deserves recognition, make sure you help spread the word about them and their work. Others start noticing when staff trusts you and knows that you celebrate the wins with them.

- Provide a safe space for your colleagues. Hold yourself accountable for being honest with them. Helping to identify gaps and empowering others to close them (without doing it yourself) is one of the best gifts you can provide.

- Consistently model leadership and recognize the leadership skills you see in others. Include others in your logic and reasoning for making leadership decisions, and know when decisions are collaborative and when they need to be made solely by you.

- Recognize that not all people want to be leaders. Allow opportunities for them to opt out if they choose. Just because they don't want to be a leader doesn't mean they don't have influence.

Following are some actions that influential leaders take to inspire people to do their best work:

- They ask colleagues what they're working on. When you do this, listen attentively and ask reflective questions to encourage people to stretch their thinking.

- If they permit you, share your own experience related to the topic. Sometimes your stories of victories and lessons learned give people tools to help them advance their own work.

- Validate and mirror their enthusiasm about the work. Your vote of confidence in their project can help them move their work beyond their expectations. If they are open to it, suggest additional resources or people they can connect with who can further inform their work.

- Have a purpose behind everything you do. As an influential Edtech Leader, you know which actions yield the most reward. When you apply your energies toward a goal, others learn what you value and follow your lead in working toward the purpose.

Edtech Leaders also contribute to ideas and serve as a mentor, working toward advancing the people with whom they work. They provide a safe space for calculated risks and understand that not all projects turn out as expected. The Savvy Edtech Leader can reflect, revise, and work to help their team do the same so that there are always lessons learned and things to do better next time. If you are directly responsible for something that did not go well, own up to it and use the pronoun "I." Conversely, if things go well and it was a team effort, use the pronoun "we," always sharing the credit and acknowledging the contributions of others.

Strong leaders are not always focused on their own gain and are willing to step aside to allow the growth and promotion of others. Sometimes your vote of support helps others find the confidence to work toward the goal. In the end, the person you support may say they didn't believe they could do it, but because you did, they were able to get across the finish line.

In many instances your goal will be to help lower barriers so that the people you support can complete their work. Some of your time will be spent assisting others in navigating processes and protocols. Your knowledge of the organization's internal workings can help people enter new situations with firm footing and help them feel more confident in unfamiliar settings.

Lowering your guard and being vulnerable by admitting mistakes, along with sharing lessons learned, invites others into safe and meaningful conversations that not only deepen trust but also serve as an example of how one can gracefully recover from projects that did not go as expected. When the people you have influenced start carrying on the processes and procedures you've helped put in place and start mirroring some of your soft skill practices, you will have become a world-class change agent. Your influence will impact many people and serve as a model for many years.

Inspire Commitment and Buy-in

As Edtech Leaders, we can all agree that the learning ecosystem has changed drastically over the past forty years. Technology is no longer an add-in or something available to only a few. Today's Edtech Leaders must explain, manage, and implement technology for all students, teachers, staff, administrators, parents, and sometimes the community at large. To be successful, you need more than instructional or technical expertise. You must know how to get buy-in and increase stakeholder commitment.

 ### *KEY STRATEGIES*

- Create a shared vision and collaborate with representative stakeholders to outline the initiative, implementation process, evaluation process, and desired outcomes. Having a shared vision that captures the purpose and goals of technology integration in the organization is critical. This shared vision should align with the organization's goals and values.

- Be transparent and provide concise communications throughout any project or implementation. Ongoing communication should be delivered in various formats.

- Solicit feedback, adjust accordingly, and communicate changes. Soliciting stakeholder feedback allows for ongoing refinement of the implementation or the desired outcomes.

- Provide timely and relevant professional development. Comprehensive professional development is vital to success and buy-in with most initiatives.

- Share success stories, giving credit where credit is due. Sharing success stories not only highlights achievements but also recognizes the efforts of those involved. Stakeholders can learn from each other's successes, encouraging the replication of successful approaches in other areas or initiatives.

Create a Shared Vision

The vision for technology integration must reflect the learning ecosystem's needs and aspirations. Involve a diverse representation of stakeholders in the decision-making process. By involving representative stakeholders in the planning stages, diverse perspectives and expertise are included. This ensures that the initiative aligns with the needs and priorities of all relevant parties and increases the sense of ownership and commitment among stakeholders. Outlining the implementation and evaluation processes alongside desired outcomes provides a road map for everyone involved. This road map helps stakeholders understand their roles, responsibilities, and expectations, leading to smoother execution and a shared understanding of the initiative's purpose. This collaborative approach helps stakeholders feel valued and respected, creating a sense of ownership and a vested interest in the success of an initiative's implementation. Always exercise a "we" mentality over an "I" mentality.

Document and communicate the progress as you reach various milestones with the planning and implementation groups and with those that will be impacted. Continually evaluate and adjust the plan based on feedback to improve the overall experience for everyone involved.

Be Transparent

Discuss the positives as well as any possible obstacles. Transparency cultivates trust among stakeholders. Discussing potential obstacles prepares stakeholders for the possible challenges ahead. When everyone knows there may be setbacks, they can brainstorm solutions and adapt strategies accordingly. This proactive approach enhances decision-making by accounting for potential risks.

Transparency in your regular updates on each initiative's progress continues the trust building. People are more likely to support when they understand and feel connected.

Customizing and personalizing communications for different groups of stakeholders is also key to ensuring that everyone is on the same page. Maintaining open communications for feedback and providing ongoing updates helps to create a collaborative environment with stakeholders. Address concerns promptly to prevent any issues from escalating. Additionally, providing an easy process for stakeholders to get assistance and help troubleshoot issues promptly will go a long way in ensuring that the project runs smoothly. By implementing these practices, stakeholders will feel valued and involved in the process, leading to a higher chance of success.

Solicit Feedback and Adjust Accordingly

Provide clear, concise communications to stakeholders before and after making adjustments. These communications prevent misunderstandings and misinterpretations. Regular updates on adjustments and progress keep stakeholders engaged and informed. Often, implementations encounter delays. When stakeholders feel involved and informed, they are more tolerant of delays and inconveniences.

Timely and Relevant Professional Development

Savvy Edtech Leaders understand that it is imperative to scaffold training efforts, tailoring them to the specific needs and goals of the individuals or groups involved. If your background is more on the technical side than the educational side, partner with curriculum leaders, technology integrationists, or select teachers to develop pedagogical strategies. Clear communication is key; by clearly outlining tangible benefits and addressing concerns, we can alleviate apprehensions and cultivate a shared understanding of the initiative's value.

Share Success Stories

From the initial vision to the impact on learning or operations, share successes with qualitative and quantitative data. Share positive ideas or feedback from those involved, including the collaboration and implementation teams, affected teachers and students, and supportive administrators. Include any positive comments from parents.

Encourage everyone involved to share their experiences. Take pictures and keep a running list of positive experiences and results, or reported challenges and strategies for overcoming them. Share the stories on multiple platforms. Before quoting someone, ask for their permission, and before posting a picture, ensure that you comply with the district's policy.

The role of an Edtech Leader has evolved to include more than organizational, instructional, and technical knowledge. A Savvy Edtech Leader must develop a shared vision, be collaborative, communicate effectively, listen, design personalized professional development opportunities, involve stakeholders in decision-making, and showcase success!

Communicate for Success

Early in her leadership career, Diane Doersch learned that people make up their own stories and insert assumptions when communication gaps exist. Rumor mills or far-fetched theories can be constructed around a project when stakeholders are not updated. How can this be avoided? Communication is one of an Edtech Leader's primary jobs.

 ## KEY STRATEGIES

- Put effort into communicating the work that you do. You can do the best work in the world, but if you are not sharing it with your audience, they will have no idea of the outstanding work your team is doing.

- Consistently communicate the progress you make on projects. Build a cadence of communication accountability so your end users receive regular updates. Doing so will prevent your audience from making up their own stories about your work.

- Use language that meets the needs of your audience. Know your audience and tailor language to their levels of understanding. Edtech Leaders know when to use precise technical language and when to "translate" the technical language into words a community member understands.

- Besides asking for feedback on your work, ask for feedback on your communication style and how it works for your audience. Make an effort to receive feedback on your communication streams and the quality of your communications. It will inform you and allow you to improve continuously.

- Less is more. Don't overburden your audience with too much information. Construct your communications so the essential information comes first in the document and more details are provided further down the page.

Edtech Leaders who excel in communication can translate complex IT topics into manageable, bite-sized pieces for their community stakeholders and talk technical with their internal staff who need clear direction. In her edtech career, Diane Doersch felt that the ability to "translate" technical concepts into digestible pieces for her board of education or school leaders was an essential skill that helped contribute to her success. Edtech Leaders must know the appropriate audience for the correct type of technical language and must discern when to code-switch and move to another language model. By listening intently, Edtech Leaders show respect and the desire to understand topics from multiple perspectives. Good communicators share information in several ways, from face-to-face conversations to short digital messages to long-form reports.

A successful communicator must anticipate the audience's needs. What questions might they have? How can you succinctly answer their questions? How can you build a loop to receive feedback on your communication so you can improve it?

Following are some additional ways Edtech Leaders can communicate for success:

Foster openness and transparency through your communications. Create an environment where team members are always welcome to share their opinions, concerns, ideas, and innovations. Having this type of culture will encourage collaboration and problem-solving.

Enlist proofreaders. Get into the habit of running your significant communications through some preliminary audiences, like a professional colleague involved in the project. Because they are familiar with the project, they can review your media for clarity and make suggestions to strengthen the message about the project. Having somebody unrelated to the project read over your messaging can also be helpful. They can raise flags when the language is too technical or too much information is provided.

Know when to withhold information. Your team members must know what they can and cannot share with others, and when. If your team has some ideas on which they are still working, avoid releasing them until they are complete.

When information is provided to the audience prematurely, it confuses end users and can shed a poor light on the department.

Answer the why. A good communicator provides appropriate context to their communications. Consider including the why so that your audience sees the big picture.

Regularly update and report. Updates are critical in long-term projects. Avoid significant communication gaps. Build a schedule for communications so your audience feels well-informed. Provide status reports, host meetings, or build presentations to update others on progress. Sharing information helps manage expectations in that people can align their expectations to the realities of the project. Include celebrations in your reports to acknowledge the people or organizations helping to make the project successful.

Nonverbal cues are essential. Communication occurs beyond the written mode. You must synchronize your body language with what you are trying to communicate. Appropriate eye contact, a smile, and confidence in your communication will help enforce the importance of the project.

Sometimes less is more in communication. Knowing when to stop talking is essential. Providing a pause for questions or for people to digest what

COMMUNICATIONS TO THE TEAM

Lucy's school district IT department had more than forty team members. Team members had various skills and roles, from data entry and new student registration to network managers and building IT technicians. Early in her leadership tenure, she created a cadence of department-wide communications to provide her team with an identity and sense of belonging. She created a weekly blog that was released to her department every Monday. The blog was a short set of paragraphs that related a work concept to her experience or a weekend adventure. Its goal was to create a sense of belonging and to make herself approachable. Eventually, other department members were invited to contribute as guest bloggers. The blogs were fun to read and created great discussion among department members. Another communication effort Lucy created was monthly department meetings. The purpose was to provide unified updates on major IT projects, district information, or departmental changes, and to celebrate birthdays and departmental accomplishments. There was always time for discussion after each piece of information was disseminated. Lucy found that when everybody heard the same vital pieces of information simultaneously, there was less confusion and employee favoritism.

you are saying is a good habit to develop. Too much information can confuse your audience and cause additional angst. Let your audience decide how much information they want to ingest once the primary bullet points are shared.

Follow up on your critical communications. Receiving feedback can help make the project stronger. You may receive new information or perspectives on your work and open up opportunities for collaboration. You can clear up misunderstandings and identify where more information is needed.

Connecting the Dots

Harnessing Trust and Intuition for Edtech Success

Capable Edtech Leaders don't rely only on strategy and charisma; they also tap into their trust and finely-tuned intuition, tools sharpened through years of professional and personal experiences. Their instincts act as their internal compass, guiding them in finding innovative solutions to intricate challenges. Instead of merely applying cookie-cutter solutions, these leaders craft novel approaches specifically tailored to their organization's unique needs. Their vast experience instills in them a confidence to spot opportunities that might elude others, turning potential obstacles into pathways for growth.

Intuitive leadership doesn't negate the value of structure. Edtech Leaders appreciate the significance of well-defined processes. Such leaders can connect the dots where others might falter, trusting that nagging idea or that gut feeling that often leads to creative outcomes. They cultivate a culture of ongoing improvement by steering their organizations from mere reactions to proactive optimization. This harmonious blend of instinctual leadership and process-driven strategies defines the essence of leadership growth, paving the way for visionary, efficient, and integrity-driven leadership.

Harnessing trust and intuition in edtech, particularly for K–12 Edtech Leaders, involves navigating a complex landscape of technological integration, cybersecurity, and effective use of educational technology. The rapid adoption of edtech, driven most recently and decisively by the COVID-19 pandemic, has significantly changed the landscape of K–12 education, presenting both opportunities and challenges for leaders in this space (Reynolds & Dhawan, 2022; CoSN, 2023; SETDA, 2023).

THE ISTE STANDARDS

This chapter connects well with the **Empowering Leader Standard (3.3)** and the **Systems Designer Standard (3.4)** from the ISTE Education Leader Standards. These standards highlight the essential balance between intuitive, trust-based leadership, and structured, process-driven strategies in educational technology.

The Empowering Leader Standard emphasizes the role of leaders in creating an environment where educators can exercise professional agency and innovation. This standard supports this chapter's theme of utilizing intuition and trust to guide decision-making and innovative problem-solving. By empowering educators and encouraging a culture of innovation and collaboration, leaders foster a setting where instinct and creativity can flourish alongside structured technological integration.

The Systems Designer Standard focuses on building robust systems and processes to support sustainable technology use. This standard complements this chapter's discussion of the importance of structured processes alongside intuitive leadership. Effective Edtech Leaders, as described in this chapter, develop and maintain systems that not only support the current technology needs but are adaptable to future challenges and innovations. This duality helps in transforming potential obstacles into opportunities for growth and ensuring that the organization's technology strategy is both efficient and adaptable.

Together, these standards encapsulate the dual nature of leadership in educational technology, where trust and intuition are balanced with rigorous system design and process optimization.

Learn to Trust Your Instincts

A quote often attributed to Ralph Waldo Emerson (but likely originated by a Wall Street trader named Henry Stanley Haskins) is "What lies beyond us and what lies before us are tiny matters compared to what lies within us." As an Edtech Leader, you must develop creative solutions to complex problems daily. Often, you are charting new paths that have yet to be traveled or at the least tweaking a previous plan to solve an ever-shifting challenge. You were selected to lead. One of the many reasons is likely because you have exhibited vision and the ability to think outside the box. You have demonstrated good judgment and well-thought-out planning.

The longer you are in an environment, the more you see and experience. These experiences shape your thoughts and provide insight into multiple points of view. As you immerse yourself into the culture, your ability to understand what is best for your environment increases. Confidence in understanding a situation and the surrounding facts allows you to capitalize on opportunities that others may not even see.

We have all experienced that *feeling*—the feeling that something may not be as it appears even though no one else feels it. We have also had the feeling that something will work when others are not connecting the dots. Most of us have had an idea in our heads that will not go away. We think about it while we are eating or trying to sleep. It is just a nagging thought. That's your gut instinct. Our gut is often referred to as our "second brain." There is a distinct difference in the way we feel when we are experiencing fear of failure versus the certainty that our gut feeling is correct. Learn the difference.

In a time when we have so much data at our fingertips, some may dismiss instinct as unreliable, "but there's a deep neurological basis for it. When you approach a decision intuitively, your brain works in tandem with your gut to quickly assess all your memories, past learnings, personal needs, and preferences, and then makes the wisest decision given the context" (Wilding, 2022).

 KEY STRATEGIES

- Determine what you are passionate about and capitalize on it. Embracing your passions allows you to tap into your natural talents and tackle your endeavors with genuine excitement.

- Reflect on your intuition as a valuable source of insight and wisdom, akin to a form of energy that can guide your decisions and actions.

- Pay attention to the subtle signals and feelings that arise within you, as they often hold valuable information about situations, people, and choices.

- As the implementation of a solution proceeds, be flexible. Tweaks are often necessary to get the best outcome.

Capitalize on Your Interests

Think of interests as your passion for an idea. If you are passionate about your work, that passion will shape your work ethic and drive. Passion fuels follow-through. The more passionate you are about an idea, the more likely your instinct is spot on!

Experience Feeds Intuition

Every good instinct follows a lot of hard work. You know how hard you study situations, observe what works, and learn from mistakes. This experience provides data points in your brain, and your instincts feed off of this data. Think of it as your brain working in concert with your gut.

Instincts Are Based on Information

You know every aspect of your department's work, the district's goals, and your organization's culture. When you become immersed in the work of your department and organization, your mind draws on all that knowledge with little effort. Your instincts are based on information. To build confidence in following your instincts, start small with decisions that are without major consequences. As you start to trust your gut instincts, you may want to analyze your thoughts for several days before responding. As you get more comfortable, you will trust your instinct more quickly and on larger issues.

Be Flexible

Test your idea on a smaller group first. When you act on an instinct, the basic idea may stay constant, but its implementation may change with input from your team, fellow Edtech Leaders, or other stakeholders. Your idea may evolve as you listen to other people's input. Permit yourself to adapt; by doing so, it will be easier to trust your instincts in the future. Fear of failure often prevents people from acting on instinct. Initial failure is more tolerable when you have listened to the ideas of others. Learning from failure and correcting your actions to produce a successful result increases your trust in your instincts.

Most of us have had a profound feeling about something but didn't know how we knew it. It might be a feeling that the timing is not right or that someone is not a good fit for your team. Listen to your instincts and learn to trust them. When your mind and gut agree, it is an extraordinary moment.

Optimize the Organization

Most leaders know their organization has room for greater efficiency. Thriving Edtech Leaders are always looking for better ways to get work done. Savvy Edtech Leaders spend the time and effort to develop processes. They know how to move the organization from a reactive, inconsistent, ad hoc state to a repeatable, defined, and optimized state. They understand that process development is one of the best ways to empower an organization to improve and innovate.

Developing processes is time-consuming and tedious. Most technologists prefer to serve staff and students rather than spend time building processes and associated documentation. As leaders, we can strive to find ways to lighten up this work and make it fun. We can present this tedious and time-consuming work as an opportunity to learn and grow. We can embed it into our organizational culture. We can use it as a method to improve continuously.

Implementing process management techniques based on total quality management principles is a great place to start, and a great example is the work from the American Productivity Quality Center (apqc.org). The APQC is the foremost authority in benchmarking, best practices, process and performance improvement, and knowledge management. Jack Grayson, former CEO of the APQC and a thought partner and mentor to many educators, blazed the trail in Process Performance Management.

Thriving Edtech Leaders research many best practices. What sets them apart is that they develop a process development strategy that works for their organization. Following is an example of a process strategy that we trust:

KEY STRATEGIES

- Understand how we get work done, who is responsible for what, and when it is done. Define the sequence of activities that provide a dynamic picture of how the organization operates at the functional level. Once a process is designed, it's easy to spot inefficiencies, deficiencies, and fragmented operations—great opportunities to innovate and improve.

- Decide on the process documentation format. Documentation may include policies, checklists, screenshots, process maps, guides, formal documentation using a template, and many other methods. There are many automated documentation tools you can consider using, as well as a variety of templates. The tools should have editing and revision capability.

- Innovate and improve the process. Essential process design is more than just documenting an existing process. It's thinking about innovating in the design process on a larger scale.

- Develop a process library. The process library is a single source of reference for all key processes. It provides a repository for staff to consult.

- Innovate and improve. Guide the team through the improvement process. Consider what steps in the process need improvement. Is the process consistent, does the process take too long, are steps duplicated, are there inefficiencies, or is unnecessary work occurring?

To Optimize, We Must Standardize

One of the quickest ways to jump-start efficiency improvement is to standardize key work processes. Standardization facilitates consistency, training, and compliance. It provides the information needed to improve the systems we have in place. Standardizing key processes may be an enormous undertaking, because technology reaches every facet of the school system.

First, we must understand the workflow and activities involved with key processes. We aren't expected to know every detail of every job. It is our responsibility to understand the key process elements and possess the skills to design new procedures that improve the effectiveness of our services.

Processes have inputs, steps, outputs, and interfaces with other established organizational processes. Processes exist to achieve results that exceed our customers' needs and expectations. Because all work processes consume resources, one aspect of work process design is eliminating steps that do not add value. Another aspect is to replicate steps that demonstrate improved efficiency. This ongoing effort is an important key to process consistency and improvement.

Definition and analysis of work processes is the key to continuous process improvement and innovation. Work processes are documented procedures defining the tools, techniques, equipment, and personnel needed to perform specific tasks. These processes establish the steps needed to execute successful and consistent work that creates value for the customer. The work process defines how work operates in your organization and allows you to evaluate effectiveness.

The Keys to Success

Identifying key processes requires deliberate effort and allocating time and resources. Organizations resist documenting work processes due to time constraints. Employees may resist the effort. Some want to hoard knowledge and skills to ensure job security. Others resist change and want to continue doing things the way they've always been done. These barriers must be overcome to build an organization that strives to improve its work.

Only you can decide which processes are crucial and warrant detailed development. Don't overthink it. Just get started. We can improve as we go. Following is one basic approach:

Form a functional-level process team. Identify the key processes related to specific areas of the organization. Consider building functional-level process teams around your organizational structure.

Develop a list of key processes. Include customers, subject matter experts, and process owners involved with each key process. This will help you know who to invite to process design meetings.

Name the key process. A key process deserves appropriate identification. The name of the key process may become part of your organization's vocabulary. Give it a meaningful label that carries energy, such as *monitoring wireless connectivity*. It's clear, specific, and action oriented.

Prioritize a list of key processes. Rank the processes that have the maximum impact on the success of your organization. When deciding what to focus on for improvement, choose the processes that deliver real value.

Set goals and define action plans. Set goals that are specific, measurable, attainable, realistic, and timely (SMART) to ensure the importance of the key process is understood.

Monitor progress. Develop a hierarchical list of key processes with categories that include functional levels, action plans, and assignees. Each work process will need a champion from the functional team to oversee and report on its improvement. Progress status is a top priority if you are serious about building work processes.

Foster Trust within Your Team

The trust of your team is not a given. Your team will compare what you say with what you do. It is easy to make promises or say things that sound good, but it is much more challenging to follow through on those promises and demonstrate a commitment to your stated goals and values. It is critical that your team trusts not only you but also each other.

Some may say, "I don't have a team or department, I am a one-person shop." A team can include others in the district or outsourced vendors. A team consists of any individuals that work with or for you to achieve the desired outcome.

 KEY STRATEGIES

- Lead by example. By exemplifying trustworthiness, transparency, respect, and reliability in every aspect, Savvy Edtech Leaders exemplify the standard for excellence and integrity, guiding their team towards shared success.

- Be consistent. Intentional planning, documentation, and communication are crucial for maintaining consistency in tone, actions, and team treatment and support.

- Create a respectful, safe, fair, and inclusive environment. Set norms for the department and communicate those norms in multiple ways until the norms become part of the department's culture.

- Engage the team. Successful Edtech Leaders engage team members in decision-making, empowering them to contribute their ideas and perspectives. They also seek regular feedback, actively listening to and addressing team members' concerns and suggestions.

- Invest time in building strong relationships with each team member. Authentic connections and a supportive environment promote trust. Show genuine interest in their well-being, both personally and professionally.

Lead by Example

As the Edtech Leader in your organization, it is critical that you demonstrate integrity, professionalism, and ethical behavior at all times.

Edtech Leaders should embody key virtues in all of their actions. Trustworthiness is foundational; ensure your words align with your deeds. Transparency follows suit, as openness and honesty in decision-making cultivate a culture of clarity and understanding. Respect is non-negotiable; valuing the opinions and contributions of each team member fuels collaboration and mutual esteem. Reliability is important in building trust between team members; be an example.

Be Consistent

Consistency in tone, actions, communications, and your team's collective and individual treatment takes intention and planning. You must document questions, appointments, conversations, processes, and procedures to ensure consistency and fairness in your actions. Prioritize follow-through. Set clear objectives and expectations for each team member. Ensure that all individuals clearly comprehend their assigned roles and responsibilities and have a complete understanding of the district's technology initiatives.

Provide equitable support and resources to ensure each team member has what they need to accomplish their tasks effectively and efficiently. Address any challenges or obstacles promptly and practice coaching strategies when applicable.

Develop consistent communication methods and meeting schedules so that team members know what to expect and when to expect it.

Create a Respectful, Safe, Fair, and Inclusive Environment

Promote a culture of open dialogue and active listening within the team, fostering an environment where everyone feels valued and at ease expressing their ideas, concerns, and feedback. Be inclusive in your language and actions, and require the same from all team members.

Address issues with individuals in private. When a "people problem" is brought to your attention, listen to all sides before giving a response beyond a simple "thanks for the heads-up." Monitor your body language to avoid showing shock, doubt, or anger. When someone reports an issue and requests complete anonymity, wait several days or weeks to call in the person involved.

Engage the Team

Successful Edtech Leaders involve team members in decision-making processes whenever possible. Motivate and empower individuals to actively contribute their unique ideas and perspectives; consider their input seriously and value their contributions. This approach fosters a sense of ownership and empowerment within the group.

Seek regular feedback from team members about their experiences, challenges, and suggestions for improvement. Actively listen to and acknowledge team members' concerns and suggestions. Take timely and appropriate actions to address them.

Invest Time in Relationship Building

To have a highly functional and effective team, it is imperative that you invest in building relationships with each member and for them to have a positive relationship with each other. Provide time for team members to build relationships. Plan team-building activities. Book studies and carefully planned professional learning activities where lunch or travel is involved provide team members with a way to get to know each other. Team building activities available on the internet vary from ice breaker questions to operation navigation to two truths and a lie—these can be fun while letting team members get to know each other as people.

Make Decisions Like a Boss

Have you ever been stuck in a never-ending cycle of non-decision-making? The work you are doing may depend on a critical decision from another team, so you are in a holding pattern until that decision is made. The decision-making group or person may need more information before somebody can set a course or direction. There may be a feeling that the decision is not important, and the situation will just work itself out. There may not be enough informed or experienced people to help make the decision, or worse yet, people may not know who the designated decision-maker is. There may be a lack of decision-making criteria, or people may not feel ready to decide.

 KEY STRATEGIES

- Decision-making is part of leadership. Know when to make a decision yourself and when to work with a collaborative group.

- Recovering from poor decisions is not impossible, but it does take intention. Acknowledging and taking ownership of your lapses in judgment goes a long way in helping build trust among your team.

- Gathering the necessary information to make the decision should be thorough. You always want to operate with the most information you can get to make an informed decision.

- Once a decision is made, communicate it well and ask for feedback. Be prepared to support your decision with data and verifiable facts.

- Work behind the scenes to gain support for the decision made. Build capacity in others to understand and implement the decision-making process so that critical decisions are supported with consistency and collegiality.

If you are a leader, you know that leadership requires making decisions. Following are some steps you can take to be an effective decision-maker:

Define the problem and goal. What problem are you trying to solve? What critical decisions will need to be made to help reach the goal? Is the decision up to you, individually? Are you expected to come to a collaborative decision? If so, who else needs to be included? If the decision needs to be made by somebody else, can your team build a recommendation?

Gather information. Collect information related to your topic. Are there experts in the field who could provide a picture of the current landscape? Have you studied the latest trends and best practices?

Identify alternatives. It may be helpful to lay out all the choices and options. Be sure to seek diverse perspectives when looking at alternatives. You may be surprised that some of your stakeholders provide the best choices because they are closest to the work.

Evaluate options. Creating a plus/delta chart that lists the decision's positives and negatives may be beneficial. Envision the plan implementation associated with the decision; what factors must be considered? You may have cost factors. You may need to do a risk analysis. Identifying the changes that need management due to the decision is also a factor to consider when examining options.

It's time to decide. Sometimes, it is hard to determine when the decision needs to be made. Who has the authority to make the decision? Have you gathered enough information and consulted enough subject matter experts to be confident in the decision?

Develop an implementation plan. Once the decision is made, you should have the details to build a robust implementation plan. Incorporate what you've learned through the information-gathering process and create an implementation plan to help you and your team meet the goals set out at the beginning. Be sure to include metrics and key performance indicators so that you can monitor the plan in its implementation stage.

Communicate the plan to others and gain buy-in. Create a complete communication plan that includes your stakeholders and end users. Share updates and critical information with those subject matter experts and peers from whom you've gathered best practices, as their experiences can help inform your implementation stage.

Monitor and evaluate. Consistently review data and gather feedback from your end users to monitor the decision's impact. Be prepared to make minor adjustments in response to the data.

Learn and iterate. Reflect on the process and encourage others to use the art of reflection to help identify what worked well, so that you can use those strategies in the future. Also, watch for the gaps identified through the reflective process and work with your team to remediate them as they arise.

You may have been plagued with the specter of poor decisions made by you or others in the past and fear moving forward. Being accountable for a poor decision is challenging. We must understand that we will only be one hundred percent successful in some of our choices. Perhaps you have made an excellent choice, but it requires better messaging and implementation. Other times, your decision may need to be corrected because it was plain wrong.

As an Edtech Leader, when you discover that you've made a poor decision, you will need to own it, acknowledge it, talk to the people adversely affected, apologize for it, remediate the situation, and then move on. Owning a poor decision with the people who have felt the consequences shows integrity. You will not forget the impact of that poor decision and will do everything you can to prevent it from happening again. Putting effort into rebuilding trust will need to be one of your priorities. Soliciting feedback during the recovery phase will help inform your work and allow all groups a voice.

LESSONS LEARNED

Diane Doersch has publicly called her less-than-stellar decisions "lessons learned." Early in her leadership career, she found the quicker she acknowledged the gaps in her decision-making, the faster she could recover. Diane said, "I have witnessed other leaders who cast blame on others to pass the buck or try to hide the poor decision, only to have the problem later blow up and impact many more people than it should. When you find yourself in that predicament, it's best to admit you made an error, own it, and work to fix it. Ensure that it truly is a "lesson learned" in that you have learned not to make that same mistake again.

10

Bridging Ideas and Actions

The Importance of Openness in Edtech Leadership

When we think of being open, we usually think of a person authentically interested in exploring new ideas, considering different perspectives, and taking an honest look at themselves. For most, learning a new skill or passing a certification test is more straightforward than figuring out how to be more open. It's easier to examine intelligence than it is to gauge openness.

Being open in an educational technology leadership position significantly affects leadership effectiveness because it influences communication, decision-making, and relationship-building. It's easy to embrace openness in the abstract, but how do we formulate a plan to be more open in our careers? What are the behavior indicators for being open? Active listening, accepting constructive feedback, and seeking advice when we are under pressure are all good indicators. Open leaders develop a commitment to lifelong learning throughout their careers (Caves, 2018).

This chapter offers guidance using real-life Edtech Leadership situations. We discuss strategies for managing emotions and boosting feelings of self-worth. In the technology landscape, inherently, there is significant uncertainty. We must be open to developing the skills we need to stay relevant and grow in the future. Being proactive in professional networking is a strategy that will mobilize your career. We all have room to grow, so why not embrace open leadership and reduce any barriers that might get in our way? The only thing that might be holding us back is ourselves.

THE ISTE STANDARDS

This chapter highlights behaviors and dispositions related to the **Connected Learner Standard (3.5)** of the ISTE Education Leader Standards, wherein leaders model and promote continuous professional learning for themselves and others. We address finding gaps in your own leadership and how to fill those gaps. We also discuss the value of networking and collaborating with others so that together you all succeed.

Let Negative Feelings Motivate You

One of the most troublesome challenges for leaders is the frustration resulting from deep feelings of inferiority. Inferiority causes some to feel less valuable or important. To others, inferiority may feel like we are not worthy of our current position. Inferiority may also cause us to think we aren't fully qualified or lack what it takes to succeed. These feelings may lead us to believe that sooner or later, others will see us for who we are, and our careers will be over.

Alfred Adler, a psychiatrist in the early 1900s, introduced the term inferiority feeling, which later became known as the inferiority complex (Adler, 1927). Throughout his practice, he developed psychotherapy methods to turn feelings of inferiority into feelings of "maturity, common sense, and social usefulness." In 1978, Pauline R. Clance and Suzanne Imes introduced a disorder called the impostor phenomenon, also known as impostor syndrome, as "an internal experience of intellectual phoniness," where we doubt our skills and capabilities (Clance & Imes, 1978). Feelings of inferiority and feeling like an imposter are very common. We encourage you to look at them as opportunities for growth. We all have room to grow. That's why you are reading this book!

KEY STRATEGIES

- Start the week by reviewing your list of goals. This review will serve as a game plan for the week. When feelings of inferiority arise, our goals will be top of mind. We can easily say, "I'm working on that" or "I have a strategy to improve myself in that area." So, when feelings of inadequacy emerge, our goals will serve as the antidote.

- Embrace feelings of inferiority. Use these feelings to keep our learning plan fresh. Inferior feelings are where the opportunities are. We can always be more creative and innovative. Use negative feelings as motivation!

- Notice any feelings of inferiority dissolving. Notice how refreshing it is. Notice when you feel more secure.

- Prepare at least five attitude adjustment statements. When feelings of inferiority creep in, say these statements to yourself confidently. Here are some examples. "I am in my position because I deserve it. I am here because of my hard work and persistence. I am worthy of my success. My unique knowledge and skills are valuable. I am the real deal!"

- Practice self-appreciation. Affirm to yourself how proud you are of what you have accomplished. Say these affirmations over and over. Know you are enough. Believe it.

When we finally reach the position we have worked and studied for, there should not be any reason to doubt ourselves. Thriving Edtech Leaders take action to conquer feelings of self-doubt. It is possible to change how we see ourselves. We must engage in positive self talk. We must take control of our thoughts.

Following are some ideas for turning self-doubt into self belief:

We know what we have accomplished. Maintain a portfolio of achievements as reminders, such as a curriculum vitae, news articles, or thank-you cards. Use these as validation to realign our reality.

Acknowledge negative feelings. Take a deep breath. Reframe the thought of self-doubt, then let it go.

Look for reasons. Ask yourself, "Why do I feel this way?" Look for patterns or situations that trigger self-doubt.

Share your feelings. Talk to allies who support us, encourage us, and lift us up. Sometimes, others can help us focus on the facts about ourselves quickly. This nudge might be what we need to fight feelings of self-doubt. We all need a confidence booster occasionally.

We are responsible for building ourselves up. Don't waste valuable energy questioning or doubting yourself. Why not spend our energy on building ourselves up? Shift negative talk in your head to positive self-talk.

Build Your Network and Connect with Others

When Sheryl Abshire was appointed as the chief technology officer for a large school district where she had been serving as an elementary school principal, the last thing on her mind was building her network. She was consumed by the daunting task ahead of her. She had to get to know her new, very small staff. She had to determine how to complete a massive infrastructure project in progress. And most importantly, she had to figure out how she would convince the superintendent and chief financial officer that she had to have more money and more staff ... fast!

She didn't believe that networking, which is sometimes thought of as the unpleasant mission of exchanging favors and cultivating relationships with strangers, was a luxury she could afford. But building her network was one of the things she began in earnest very quickly.

Networking is defined by Herminia Ibarra and Mark Lee Hunter in the *Harvard Business Review* as "creating a fabric of personal contacts who will provide support, feedback, insight, resources, and information. [It] is simultaneously one of the most self-evident and one of the most dreaded developmental challenges that aspiring leaders must address" (Ibarra & Hunter, 2007).

 ### KEY STRATEGIES

- Build relationships. Networking is about creating meaningful relationships rather than accumulating contacts. Take the time to understand people, their interests, and how you can help each other.

- Actively engage. Regularly engage with your network through sharing helpful information, reaching out for a casual check-in, or participating in discussions. Engaging regularly keeps relationships strong and ensures you're remembered.

- See a mutual benefit. Always approach networking with the intention of mutual benefit. Networking should never be a one-sided relationship where you're always asking for favors. Aim to give as much as you take.

- Diversify. Expand your network beyond your immediate field or industry. A diverse network can provide unique perspectives, opportunities, and connections that might not be available within your field.

- Be consistent and persistent. Effective networking requires time and patience. Keep connecting and engaging with people even when the benefits aren't immediately apparent. With persistence, the value of your network will grow over time.

Michele Jennae, a well-known creativity coach, tells us networking is more than connecting people. It's about connecting people with people, people with ideas, and people with opportunities. Edtech Leaders often rise to their positions by being good at their jobs and focusing on team goals. When asked to look at more significant issues, they might struggle because they need to be more sociable, not just analytical. They must interact with different people within and outside their organization. These interactions aren't distractions but core parts of their new roles. Many new leaders feel networking is fake or selfish, and some find it hard to overcome this idea. But without networking, they risk failing to succeed in a leadership role.

Three kinds of networking are crucial: operational, personal, and strategic. Operational networking helps leaders manage current tasks. Personal networking boosts their development. Strategic networking opens up new opportunities and connects them with necessary stakeholders. Unfortunately, most leaders under-value strategic networking.

Operational Networking

Leaders need to establish good relations with those who can help them accomplish tasks. This network should include immediate superiors, subordinates, equals in the department, other internal stakeholders, and key external people. Your goal should be to ensure cooperation among people who need to trust each other to complete tasks. Even if difficult, it's straightforward because the task provides focus.

Despite being natural for most leaders, operational networking can have blind spots. Relying solely on operational networks can be limiting because they focus on current tasks rather than strategic goals. These networks are primarily dictated by job roles and organizational structures and typically stay within the organization, centered on short-term demands.

As new Edtech Leaders step into their roles, their networks need to look outward and ahead. It's easy to be more focused on maintaining current networks than preparing for future challenges. As a new leader, your networks must also focus on external interactions and future-oriented goals.

Once leaders realize focusing too much internally is a risk, they start connecting externally with like-minded people in their field. However, they often need knowledge outside their field. Joining professional associations, alumni groups, and personal interest communities can give them new perspectives that aid their career growth. This is known as personal networking.

Personal Networking

Some Edtech Leaders question the value of investing time in activities not directly related to work. Why expand casual contacts when even simple tasks can be overwhelming? The answer lies in the valuable referrals, information, and support these contacts provide. For example, as a new education CTO and facing numerous critical situations, Sheryl Abshire joined a business technology group with her local Chamber of Commerce. She met a group of technology professionals who helped her navigate through issues that needed more expertise than she had at the time. Her success led her to network with other public and private sector technology professionals in her community and grow in her expertise and prowess.

Personal networks are also a safe space for personal growth and can lay the groundwork for strategic networking. Personal networks are usually external, consisting of voluntary connections with people who share something in common. Their power lies in their referral potential—the idea that our contacts can help us reach the person with the information we need in as few steps as possible. As Edtech Leaders strive to expand their professional relationships, we often see them shift their focus from operational to personal networking. This is a crucial first step for those who have yet to look outside their organizations. However, more than personal networking is needed to help you become a leader. You may find new interests or gain influence in a professional community but need help to engage with higher-level power players or link these connections to organizational goals.

Personal networking will only aid a leadership transition if these connections are used strategically.

Often leaders who think they are adept at networking operate only at an operational or personal level. Influential leaders also learn to employ networks for strategic purposes.

Strategic Networking

Edtech Leaders must understand broad strategic issues. Connecting with other leaders outside their direct control helps them know how their work fits into the larger picture. This type of connection is called strategic networking, and it's essential for achieving personal and organizational goals.

An Edtech Leader's job is to set the direction and bring in the necessary people and groups. This involves recruiting stakeholders, diagnosing the political landscape, and fostering discussions among unrelated parties. Some leaders recognize their increasing reliance on others and seek to convert it into mutual influence, while others avoid what they see as "political" work, hindering their progress. Not understanding that most organizations and certainly school districts have clear political underpinnings at work can cost a leader their influence and potentially career stability and growth.

An excellent strategic network leverages information, support, and resources from one area to achieve results in another. Strategic networkers indirectly influence their environment, shaping it in their favor. However, strategic networking can be challenging because it takes a lot of time and energy that leaders usually use for operational tasks.

Operational, personal, and strategic networks can coexist. For example, a leader can use a hobby to meet people from various professions. Even though these new friends aren't related to your work, their experiences in the community can offer a fresh perspective on your work. What starts as a personal network can become operationally and strategically valuable. It's important to let strategic needs guide relationship building, and not just personal chemistry.

Networking is part of work, and it can be challenging. It often means stepping out of your comfort zone. So, how can Edtech Leaders make networking less daunting and more beneficial? The answer lies in mixing different types of networking—for example, using personal contacts for strategic advice or turning colleagues into allies. But the first step is to change how you think about networking.

Leaders often say, "I'm too busy for networking." Some see networking as an unfair way to get things done, favoring "who you know" over "what you know." When future leaders don't see networking as a vital part of their new role, they won't dedicate enough time and effort to make it worthwhile.

A good role model can be the best solution to this problem. Sometimes, observing someone you respect who networks effectively and ethically can change your perspective. Networking is about judgment and intuition, which we can develop by observing and learning from others who do it well.

Some Edtech Leaders think a good network involves having many contacts or attending big events. But we've seen people start networking by organizing their contacts, only to fail at the crucial next step: reaching out. The best networkers continually engage with their network, whether they need help or not. A network is only valuable when it's active. A great start can be making a simple request or introducing two people who could benefit from getting to know each other. Taking action gets things moving and shows you can contribute.

You have to stick with it. The benefits of networking take time to develop. Many leaders plan to network more, only to be put off by the first hurdle they face. Building a leadership network is about commitment, not skill. When the initial efforts don't show quick results, some people conclude they're not good at networking. But networking isn't a natural talent, nor does it require being outgoing. It's a skill you can learn with practice.

Networking today doesn't mean you have to be in the same room with people. Commenting on or sharing LinkedIn posts of people in your network, meeting virtually, or reaching out to contacts via text for a quick hello are all great ways to keep your network alive. Technology has democratized and flattened out the world, and we now have easy access to the people in our networks. Why not use it? Savvy Edtech Leaders must redefine themselves, develop new relationships, and acknowledge that networking is crucial to their new roles.

Future-Proof Your Organization

Future-proofing is the proactive approach of anticipating and preparing yourself for future changes and challenges to minimize their impact. It includes the evaluation of future trends and potential threats, while also devising plans and methods to mitigate them. By embracing future proofing, organizations can foresee, adjust to, and even embrace these changes, guaranteeing their success and continued relevance.

Handling uncertainty is challenging, but adapting is vital to doing well, especially during significant changes. Edtech Leaders must be able to handle complex, high-pressure situations. To prepare your organization for the future, overcoming the habit of falling back to what we're used to when stressed is essential. Instead of just recovering from tough times, learn to move ahead better than before. Ask yourself what skills are important for your plans and how your team and tools can work together to build those skills.

 ## *KEY STRATEGIES*

- Stay informed about global changes that could impact your work.

- Keep an eye on trends that could affect your organization and career.

- Identify your top strength, understand its significance, and leverage it for future success.

- Recognize your primary weakness, understand how it might limit you, and devise strategies to address it.

- Regularly assess the skills and competencies required for the future workplace, and if necessary, start developing them now.

The COVID-19 pandemic strongly impacted organizations of every size and type. Even before COVID-19, technology had transformed work and the skills needed to succeed. The pandemic disrupted efforts to close these skill gaps. The focus shifted from finding new talent to survival. But as organizations continue to recover from the pandemic, those that upgrade their workforce for the future will outdo their competitors. Even before working remotely was standard, digital technology was changing where, how, and by how many people work was done. Predictive analytics and generative AI may reduce the workforce needed, altering required skills and enabling remote work.

Future-proofing is a big task for Edtech Leaders. Organizations will need new tech, talent, partnerships, tools, and financial strategies. Leaders must improve their skills, focusing more on motivating, mentoring, and supporting important roles instead of just controlling information, and building solid cultures within and outside the organization. They'll also need to help their teams navigate significant changes.

Not all jobs are of equal importance. Research by Bain and Company (Allen, Root, & Schwedel, 2017) shows that less than five percent of organizational roles contribute to more than ninety-five percent of its success. As the pandemic continues to redefine productivity, organizations must identify critical skills for a tech-focused future, develop these in existing employees, and actively recruit for them.

To future-proof your organization, you need to rethink what success means. Not too long ago, traditional ways of evaluating employees' work were focused on positions that didn't change much over time. Today, you must understand that the positions you supervise, as well as your own, will likely evolve quickly. Our ideas about essential skills and what success means must also evolve. With this evolution in mind, create talent development and hiring plans. Encourage employees to learn new skills through training and coaching. After the pandemic, how we work and define success must change. You'll need to hire people who can adapt to the new normal.

In tough times, organizations might want to cut training budgets. Future-proofed organizations prioritize manager and leadership training. Despite the pandemic easing some job markets, many roles are still hard to fill. Top organizations are "reskilling": teaching current valued employees new skills. Many of an organization's future roles could be filled by current employees with the right training. It's also much cheaper and more effective than hiring. Hiring new talent can be expensive, especially for jobs in high-demand areas like technology. Consider teaching current employees new skills before searching for new people who already have them.

It's critical to know what your future top employees want. The needs of tomorrow's leaders have changed compared to a decade ago. According to the Deloitte Global 2022 Gen Z and Millennial Survey report, millennials will make up a significant portion of the workforce by 2030, and their prioritization of flexibility, diversity, engagement, autonomy, and close relationships with their employers will be a critical component of their career (Deloitte, 2022). The key to retaining and inspiring employees is building an inclusive culture and efficient work settings and rewarding dedicated employees.

More than just a good salary, future workers want a strong connection with their employer's mission. They want to join an organization that makes a positive impact. They desire a sense of belonging in a culture that motivates them to do their best. Additionally, successful organizations embrace diversity and inclusion. Diversity is not just a hiring issue; it should be a crucial aspect of your talent plan.

In their book *Stretch: How to Future-Proof Yourself for Tomorrow's Workplace*, authors Karie Willyerd, Barbara Mistick, and Joseph Grenny discuss the seven trends that are shaping workers' futures: globalization, demographic changes, data growth, new technologies, climate change, changing jobs, and complexity (Willyerd, Mistick, & Grenny, 2016). In their book, they say these trends are reshaping the future of work and may make many professionals outdated. Consequently, the only way to stay relevant in the future is to adapt and grow with these changes. But where do we start? Whether we plan for it or not, careers will evolve, and the best way to prepare for change is to understand yourself better.

For individuals, self-reflection and awareness can be the best way to improve and stay relevant. For organization leaders, promoting self-awareness can create a culture of continuous learning and secure their organization's place in the future work scene.

Network via Associations

Networking is the best way to find a good or a better job fast. Most of the best jobs are taken before they're even advertised. Networking is the best and sometimes the only way to get a good job, especially when companies aren't hiring. So, where can you go if you're new to networking? Try professional groups or organizations. There are professional groups for almost every job or interest out there. You should be able to find at least one or two. These groups exist to help their members with things like legal support, setting job standards, and networking. Joining a professional group is an excellent way to keep up with what's happening in your job field and to learn about the latest trends and job opportunities.

 KEY STRATEGIES

- Join relevant professional associations. Becoming a member of industry-specific associations can provide access to resources, events, and networking opportunities that align with your career goals.

- Engage in association activities. Don't just be a passive member. Participating in association events, webinars, and conferences will help you to stay updated on industry trends and establish meaningful relationships.

- Leverage professional networks. Set up strong network profiles that represent your professional journey accurately. Use them to connect with peers, potential employers, and mentors, and engage with industry-specific groups to broaden your network and visibility.

- Seek endorsements and give recommendations. Endorsements on professional networks validate your skills and add credibility to your profile. Similarly, endorsing and recommending others can strengthen your relationships within your network.

- Expand your network strategically. Start with a small network of trusted contacts and gradually connect with professionals in your industry. Your goal should be to build a diverse network that can provide different perspectives and opportunities.

Professional associations provide opportunities for Edtech Leaders to connect with colleagues and other professionals in the field. They often allow you to meet new people, learn, and advocate for issues and concerns common to you and other like-minded colleagues. Professional groups stand up for their members and help to improve their work. They also ensure that everyone in their field follows established professional rules. These associations often provide networking opportunities, offer continuing education options, and provide resources such as job boards and scholarly journals. Clay Shirky, vice provost for AI and Technology in Education at NYU, tells us, "It's not just about delivering content to members; it's about the convening power to help members discover each other."

Is it really worth joining professional associations? Check their websites for membership details, benefits, and costs to see if a professional group is worth joining. Joining a professional group can be very useful for people already working or wanting to work in a particular field. You can meet and learn from others who do the same work; sometimes, the group may offer discounts on things like insurance. Also, experts write articles for the group's academic magazines, website, and other publications. If you need extra education credits to keep your professional license or certification, these groups often offer online and in-person classes to help you meet these needs. Being part of a professional group gives you access to unique resources, academic magazines, and a chance to meet possible employers. It can also help you decide whether to work in a particular field. Being part of such a group can help you gain experience, make friends you'll know for life, and build your resume. In fact, the four authors of this book met in a professional organization and have become lifelong friends and colleagues!

Another advantage of being part of an association is that you can attend special events like conferences and seminars only for members. At these events, many professionals meet, either in person or online. They listen to important talks and chat with other professionals. The latest news and information is shared. People can look at the event schedule to see if it matches their career goals and interests. Members might not have to pay to get into these events. Some employers pay for their employees to attend these events due to the professional learning and opportunities these events offer.

So, you've joined an association; what are your next steps? First, you should join the association mailing lists and groups. Edtech Leaders should first look to the International Society for Technology in Education (ISTE, iste.org) and the Consortium for School Networking (CoSN, cosn.org) as professional Edtech Leadership associations. These mailing lists and groups keep you updated on what's happening in your industry and when the association is meeting or having events. These events are perfect for networking. Next, consider using a network like LinkedIn to network with other association members. LinkedIn is a platform that allows job seekers to connect with other professionals. Most professionals today have a LinkedIn profile or a similar network profile. Following are five easy steps to help you network effectively using a professional network such as LinkedIn, Meetup, Xing, Bark, Opportunity, Jobcase, or Lunchmeet:

1. Create a relevant profile with a current picture: Your profile is like an online resume. It should reflect your experience, education, and career goals. If you're looking for jobs in technology, your profile should show your knowledge and involvement in that field.

2. Start making connections: LinkedIn and other networks allow you to connect with other members. Start by connecting with people you know, like friends, family, and coworkers. These people form a basis for expanding your network later.

3. Ask for endorsements: After creating a network, start requesting endorsements. Endorsements validate your skills and make connecting with others in your industry more accessible.

4. Expand your network:

   - Once you have a small network and some endorsements, add more connections.

   - Check out the connections of your existing contacts and invite them to join your network.

   - Be strategic and thoughtful and take your time increasing your network to avoid being penalized by LinkedIn or other platforms for adding too many people too fast.

5. Join LinkedIn or another professional group: After growing your network, join relevant professional groups on LinkedIn or other networks. These groups can give you additional credibility and opportunities for self-promotion. Ensure your profile aligns with the groups you request to join to increase your chances of acceptance.

Create a Pathway for Change

Our technological world is changing and advancing daily. It has pushed humans to grow with it or become obsolete. Diane Doersch always says that technology is the easy part; it's just 0s and 1s put together into unending combinations. It's the humans who have a hard time in our changing world—because adapting, revising, and reinventing does not seem to come easy to people.

An Edtech Leader can help promote change and create pathways for it. You may know of a leader who is good at creating organizational changes. They most likely articulate a clear vision of their goals in making the change. They have been good at analyzing root causes and finding many ways to improve processes or systems. They can effectively communicate the need for a particular change. They may have built a coalition of people who can identify the root causes of problems in a system and then help develop convincing reasons why the organization needs to change. They have probably created a change management plan (you will learn how to create one later in this section) and provide training and support to help end users adapt.

KEY STRATEGIES

- Change is a constant in the IT world. Communicating, planning for, and adapting to change are skills you will have to develop. Learn from each change management experience.

- Root cause analysis is essential in identifying where the "breakdowns" are in current processes. Spend a significant amount of time on this step to understand where the issues lie before you create solutions. If you are not intentional about this step, you might be fixing the wrong thing.

- Communication throughout the whole change process can make or break your success. Don't let an excellent product be foiled by a poor execution strategy. Have an intentional communication plan explaining why the change is needed and how your end users will benefit.

- Encourage multiple perspectives during the whole change process, including representatives of the people whom the change will impact. Talking directly to the people impacted by the existing poor process will help provide many perspectives on the problem and why it is a problem.

- Have frequent check-ins during the change process and make minor adjustments when necessary. Listen closely to your end users before, during, and after implementing the change. Gather benchmark data and have conversations about what the data is showing.

Diane Doersch remembers when they facilitated a change in their staff's classroom computer workstation. "The old desktop computers, monitors, and keyboards were permanently placed on teachers' desks with the ethernet cable plugged into the back. Many of the desktops also had Voice over IP (VoIP) phones plugged into them. We had heard for years that some teachers were unhappy with classroom arrangement options because their desks had to be located close to where the ethernet drop was installed in the classroom. This reality greatly limited options to lay out a room to meet the needs of students. Eventually, the need to upgrade teacher workstations provided the opportunity to help manage a significant change, where teacher voices could be heard along with the technology department in finding the best solution. Our teachers requested portable devices that allowed them to move about the classroom, providing proximity to their students. They wanted the freedom to take their devices home and also asked that we provide a docking station so that they could easily connect classroom sound and video equipment to it. While they were initially unhappy with moving from a larger monitor to a laptop screen, over time most teachers felt the portability was worth the change. Our department of technology planned to economically standardize the devices so that repairs and professional learning could be designed specifically for the device.

"Our department of technology talked extensively with many departments, including curriculum, facilities, adaptive technology, and special education. They also consulted with students and teachers to get an initial feel for what teachers wanted the new devices to do for them and their classrooms. We then talked with our vendor partners and provided them with baseline specs. Our solution providers donated sample devices, which we took on a road show to all four quadrants of our school district. We invited teachers to attend an open house and gave demonstrations on each device. We gathered feedback from staff members to find the most helpful laptop device. By the time we made the purchase, we had the support and excitement of the teachers—important in getting them to embrace and train on the new devices.

"The move from desktops to laptops was successful because we all had a clear vision for what we wanted: to enhance the classroom teaching experience by providing an easy-to-use, portable, and accessible device to teachers. We communicated with our staff every step of the way regarding purpose, the information we learned from our listening sessions, what we learned from our teachers, what our base specs needed to be, and when teachers could attend the laptop preview sessions to provide feedback on them. Our team members were vigilant in listening to and identifying ongoing classroom concerns. We collaborated with other departments to ensure that we had created the best road show experience and process for device orientation when the time came. Through our approach, we gained teacher buy-in and support, which helped make a potentially difficult change straightforward."

Not all changes will occur that successfully, but with a clear vision, careful planning, and communication, the execution of a change can be much easier.

Following are things you will want to include in your change management plan:

Find the root cause of the problem. Root cause analysis is a systemic way to identify the underlying reasons for a problem.

Define the change. Clearly articulate what change will take place. You may not know the specifics at the beginning of the change process, but always having your end goal in mind will help you identify the changes needed to reach that goal.

Assess the current state. Document the reasons why the change needs to happen. What is the current reality, and what things can or will go wrong if the change is not made? What is the cause of the problem? What is the desired state?

Create a team to manage the change. Invite team members closest to the broken process to participate in the root cause analysis and solution seeking. Also consider including skeptics, influential change-makers, and the quiet, efficient workers who like to get things done.

Develop a communication strategy. Keep communication at the forefront. Document the current reality and the proposed future state so that when employees ask why the change needs to take place, your answer is readily available. Go to stakeholders and end users often to receive feedback and identify gaps.

Plan and prepare the implementation. Never let poor communication or execution spoil a great plan. Develop a detailed change management plan, including timelines, milestones, and resource requirements. Identify and address ahead of time any risks and challenges you foresee. Ensure you have created and offered professional learning around the topic so your staff will be ready for the change.

Execute the change. Roll out the change according to your plan. Consistently monitor and keep track of benchmarks. Report them often. Create opportunities for continuous feedback and make revisions to the plan when necessary.

Evaluate and sustain the change. Evaluate the change against the key performance indicators you initially created. Consistently gather feedback from your end users and those implementing the change. Be willing to refine and adjust as you go, and always tie the goals of the change into the strategic plans of your district.

Celebrate success. Take time out throughout the project to stop and celebrate your accomplishments. Acknowledge the efforts and contributions of all who assisted.

Learn and improve. Capture lessons learned. Keep documentation of your change process, as you may want to bring new changes forward using this model.

Rising Above

The Role of Resilience and Respect

bserving organizations, especially Edtech Leaders, is fascinating in challenging times. Some can adapt, whether it be to a pandemic, budget cuts, or technological advances. Some can manage their stress. Others sink into a slump. When things get tough or are out of their control, they find leading and inspiring others more challenging. The character trait of resilience is the distinguishing factor in those with an innate ability to rise and meet whatever challenges come their way.

In thinking about resilience, one formal definition from *Merriam-Webster* is "the capability of a strained body to recover its size and shape after deformation caused mainly by compressive stress." Successful Edtech Leaders are able to do much more than recover. The most successful emerge stronger after experiencing challenges.

Observe any thriving leader. They radiate a resilient, respectful presence. When people respect you as a person, they admire you. When they respect you as a friend, they love you. When they respect you as a leader, they follow you. The opposite is true as well. As soon as people lose respect for you, your influence over them will disappear (Maxwell, 2022).

The best leaders influence us so that we feel calmer, knowing we can recover from whatever challenge comes our way. They offer a bastion of support that makes everyone around them believe it will be okay. They know how to put things in order by removing obstacles and minimizing chaos. They build resiliency reserves that help the organization stay afloat when times become difficult.

Resilient people look forward and take an active approach to facing challenges. Most importantly, they are made, not born (Stejskal, 2023). Building resiliency and respect is not a solitary journey. It's about surrounding ourselves with experts and tapping into the wisdom of other successful leaders. This support network is crucial in helping us find the strength to move through any challenge that comes our way, making us feel supported and part of a community.

THE ISTE STANDARDS

Chapter 11 connects to many ISTE Education Leader Standards. Don't successful Edtech Leaders reflect the Standards of **Equity and Citizenship Advocate (3.1)**, **Visionary Planner (3.2)**, **Empowering Leader (3.3)**, **Systems Designer (3.4)**, and **Connected Learner (3.5)**? The strategies in this chapter inspire us to consider a new perspective focused on believing in a better future. Resilience is a decision. As challenging events occur, we decide to move forward. We acquire methods that we practice before any adversity occurs and do not wait until something happens. Reaching this level requires us to work in advance in a disciplined, mindful way.

Learn About GRIT

What do you think the number one predictor of success is? You might say talent, level of education, interpersonal skills, or intelligence. One predictor is GRIT (Guts, Resilience, Initiative, Transformation). Grit is enduring the work that must be done when others give up.

KEY STRATEGIES

- Visualize your daily goals through the lens of your long-term goal. When it comes to reaching any goal, visualization is key. We must see ourselves achieving the goal to make it a reality.

- For your top three daily goals, create a sense of urgency, balanced with a sense of purpose. Urgency does not mean emergency. And at the same time, create a sense of purpose aligned with your long-term goal.

- Be decisive. Every time we face a decision, say assertively, "Yes," "No," "I don't know," or "I will give it consideration." Don't hesitate. We can always change our minds later. Don't be the leader that agonizes over a decision.

- Turn every challenge or setback into an opportunity. Reflect, learn, and move forward with a better plan.

- Lead the way. Be creative. In every task, goal, challenge, or idea, find a way to lead the effort and get the work done. No excuses.

Grow Your GRIT

We can grow our GRIT:

G is for Guts. It takes guts to step up and be the leader. It takes guts for us to step out of our comfort zone and say, YES, we can do this. It takes courage to go beyond the ordinary and be extraordinary.

R is for Resilience. Resilience is what keeps us coming back. Keep moving forward. Keep showing up again and again and again. We must develop the mindset that we will recover from any setback and adjust quickly to whatever comes our way.

I is for Initiative. Initiative is the capacity to activate the energy of action. It's taking the first step towards getting something done, independently of outside influence or control.

T is for Transformation. To transform anything, we must use our energy to boost our stamina. We must see things through without quitting, with a longer-term goal in mind. When there are challenges, embrace them, knowing that everything is a learning experience.

Nitty Gritty Leadership

Be assertive but not aggressive. Aggressiveness, especially for women, comes across as being bossy. Talk more than others, but at the right time. Those who speak first and most are usually seen as leaders and the most influential. Those who speak last are seen as closers and also hold power.

Cross your arms when you talk about something important. Crossing your arms sends a message of confidence. Do this when a decision is to be made, or a controversial subject is to be discussed.

Use positive self-talk. Leaders that make encouraging statements to themselves maintain the highest levels of performance. If you are getting ready to speak in front of a group, take a deep breath and say, "I can do this; I've prepared myself for this moment."

If you are not sure whether to sit down or stand up, stand up. This is especially crucial if you are a new leader. Standing up signals you are in charge. It encourages others to accept your authority. If you sit, sit at the head of the table. If working virtually, arrive at the conference several minutes early.

Be willing to delegate and give away some of your power or status, but ensure everyone knows it was your choice.

Others Can Help You Grow Your GRIT

Look for energizers to support you. High performers create enthusiasm for things. They create energy, which generates high performance and gets other people engaged in and supportive of their actions.

People can affect energy and enthusiasm in various ways. Interactions with some people can leave you feeling drained, while others can leave you feeling enthused about possibilities. Enthusiasm is a predictor of high performance. The most successful teams and organizations have networks filled with interconnected energizers. Energizers are engaging, value others' ideas, and help people feel like they are making progress.

Focus on the details. Organizations are filled with time-consuming and distracting routines that could be more manageable. More important things can fall through the cracks in making deadlines, going to meetings, and getting through red tape. Allocate time to show people you care. A quick break for food or fun is always welcome.

Protect yourself from the energy suckers; spend as little time around them as possible. If we can't escape the downers we lead or work with, do what you must, but train yourself to care less about all of their opinions. Save your passion and creativity for those who will benefit from it and leave you feeling charged rather than drained. Developing the fine art of indifference and emotional detachment is part of becoming a great leader.

Hunker Down and Be the Leader

GRIT gets you there. Work persistently through challenges, maintaining effort and interest despite failure, adversity, and plateaus in progress. Based on the following quote often attributed to him, Albert Einstein saw himself as gritty rather than brilliant: "It's not that I am so smart; it is just that I stay with my problems longer."

Give your team more credit than you believe they deserve. Give your people as much credit as possible and take as little as possible yourself. You get tons of credit anyway because you are the leader. Your people will see you as more truthful, and you will be admired for your modesty and generosity.

Decisions and prioritization don't wait for the picture to be clarified. We often must make decisions on the fly.

We must keep our spirits up even if we don't fully know what we are doing. By acting as if we know what we are doing and are in control, even if it isn't true at first, we reassure our followers and ourselves. As the old saying goes, fake it until you make it. Acting confident makes us feel confident—belief follows behavior. Confidence is necessary because, like many emotions, it is contagious and will spread to those who look to us for leadership.

Minimize Chaos

In our technology-dependent world, the potential for chaos is always on the horizon. The organization's needs and wants are constantly changing and growing. Cybersecurity threats, safety, funding, refresh plans, curriculum adoptions, building projects, personnel changes, and the unknown can lead to chaos if changes is not carefully planned, communicated, and implemented.

Incremental changes are required to maintain the status quo; transformative changes cause significant shifts in how people work and learn. It is imperative that implementers of change and those affected by the change understand why the change is necessary and how it will affect them.

 KEY STRATEGIES

- With any major change initiative, get input from all stakeholders and create a road map or plan that incorporates that input. Get input from not just those affected by the change but also from those who will be doing the work.

- Change initiatives will generally encounter resistance from various members or groups of members from the learning community. Recognize the resistance and develop a plan to address it.

- Offer comprehensive assistance and guidance to all stakeholders not only during the initial implementation phase but also in the post-implementation period to ensure a smooth transition and sustained success. This support should include addressing concerns, providing necessary resources, and facilitating training or education to promote understanding and proficiency with the new systems or processes.

Incorporate Stakeholder Input

As with all your work, implementing change should align with the organization's vision and overarching goals. Begin with the alignment as you develop the plan. Define the project's scope and why the change is needed.

Note who will lead each step along the way in the plan. Work with all departments and locations to discuss how the change will affect their work or any initiatives they have planned.

Paint a concise, clear picture of what success looks like, and outline the steps to get there. Communicate the road map to all affected stakeholders.

Addressing Resistance

There are generally two reasons change is needed: one, something is not working, or two, proactive future-proofing. The type of need typically determines the time-table, scope of change, and scale of resistance. The "not working" category can range from "we're not reaching our goals" to "we're in big trouble." It can also have many drivers, such as insufficient bandwidth for online testing, inability to adequately track absenteeism, remote learning crashing, a cyberattack, or any other system going down. Perhaps your predecessor hasn't kept up with changing needs or best practices. Generally, the "not working" need is more visible and encourages less resistance than proactive future-proofing. When implementing proactive future-proofing change, communicate a clear picture of the vulnerabilities or issues that will likely occur without the changes. Clear and frequent communication builds trust. The unknown breeds fear, and fear intensifies resistance.

Engage all stakeholders before, during, and after the change. Be positive but honest about timetables, inconveniences, and hiccups. Transparency builds trust. The best rule of thumb for any Edtech Leader is to under promise and over deliver. In other words, set reasonable expectations and finish ahead of schedule or under budget. Outline when and how the change will occur. With your team, discuss who will do what and provide the tools and support they need to succeed. Listen to your team and all affected stakeholders. Hear the fear. Outline the benefits of the end results. Address the concerns in a positive manner, eliminating defensive language.

Build a coalition of change advocates. Some will always believe that the current landscape is working and will have a "don't rock the boat" mentality. Change advocates can help shift that mentality. Seek out stakeholders who see the big picture and can work as advocates for the change. Make sure they have accurate information and keep them up-to-date and involved. Tag individuals who are well respected and trusted in the organization. These influencers can keep you informed of concerns you may not otherwise know about.

Support Stakeholders

It is critical to keep all stakeholders informed and to monitor people's emotions. Throughout the process, there will be low and high points for both those implementing the change and those affected by the change. Leaders must align people to the reason for the change, often working against long-standing habits and beliefs.

Utilize a project management tool. Whether it is a spreadsheet, document template, or specific application, you need a consistent way to create a timeline with action steps and responsible parties. Track expenditures to ensure that you remain within budget.

Follow up with all departments and locations to minimize disruption in their day-to-day work. Avoid working in isolation. Keep track of what is happening throughout the organization and plan accordingly.

Chunk the implementation steps into a series of phases. Celebrate the completion of each phase. Have scheduled check-ins with all parties involved with the implementation work. This includes any tasks that are outsourced. Be fluid in handling issues as they arise. Expect the unexpected: contractors not showing up, delays in product shipments, inclement weather closings, etc.

Revisit the road map after each phase to ensure everything is on target and getting the desired results. If the road map needs adjusting, take the necessary actions and communicate the changes to stakeholders. As with much of what Edtech Leaders do, planning and communication are key to success!

Earn the Respect of Others

Earning the respect of others is no easy task. It doesn't always come naturally, and it certainly doesn't come with the job. Respect must be earned, especially in a leadership position. It's essential that the people you work with respect you as a person, and not just as a leader.

Gaining the respect of employees is a crucial component of becoming an effective leader. Listening to others and respecting their differences, beliefs, and opinions indicates that you are caring and concerned. Taking the time to understand the thoughts, experiences, and views of others is a critical aspect of earning their respect. Fostering an environment conducive to respectful listening creates a workplace open to ideas and varying opinions.

 KEY STRATEGIES

- Be open to change. To earn respect, and effectively evolve and grow as a leader, you must be open to change, embracing new ideas and continually learning. This adaptability not only fosters personal growth but also creates a respectful and dynamic atmosphere.

- Be a good listener. Your body language plays a significant role in showing your attentiveness. It's important to fully focus on what is being said, rather than merely waiting for your turn to speak. Using the acronym WAIT—Why Am I Talking?—can remind you to listen more thoughtfully and to earn respect by understanding when to speak and when to listen.

- Be respectful. Acting respectfully, demonstrating compassion, and avoiding gossip help ensure that others value and respect you. Speaking up against disrespect further reinforces that respect is a fundamental norm in the workplace.

- Be transparent. Be honest with employees about their roles and what is expected of them, ensuring transparency in all organizational decisions and job expectations. This openness builds respect and trust in your leadership, as employees clearly understand what to expect.

- Be fair. To build respect and elicit trust from your team members, you must provide the same support to everyone and avoid favoritism. Making sure all employees feel equally valued supports workplace morale and avoids feelings of workplace injustice.

Author Kenneth Blanchard tells us that the key to successful leadership today is influence, not authority. Gaining respect from your employees begins with demonstrating that you value them and prioritize their growth. Prioritize communication with employees and take the time to explain and discuss important decisions. Nurturing an environment that focuses on employee respect supports workplace morale. It can create greater worker satisfaction and motivation for employees to be more productive.

How do you gain respect from employees? Influential leaders earn the respect of their employees by promoting and standing up for their best interests and offering robust and professional leadership. While it's important that your employees respect you, it's just as important that you show them the respect that they deserve. Respect is a two-way street. Show employees you respect them through your words and, more importantly, through your actions.

Exhibiting a solid work ethic sets an example for the rest of the team. Not asking more of your employees than you are willing to do builds trust and indicates that you are a reliable and hardworking leader. Being selfless in your work, doing what is necessary, and expecting nothing in return will build trust and respect.

Making decisions is a critical component of being a robust and effective leader. However, it's a foregone conclusion that not everyone will agree with your decisions. To build trust and respect with your employees and other leaders, you must make decisions based on the organization's best interests rather than on popularity. You won't build trust and respect by avoiding conflict or confrontation.

As a respected and admired Edtech Leader, you should have nothing to hide. Be straightforward with good news and bad. Endeavor not to make promises lightly. Leaders are human, and you will occasionally make mistakes. What's important is that you readily admit your mistakes and, by example, demonstrate to your employees how to bounce back from a mistake.

Respect the thoughts and opinions of your employees and other leaders in your organization. Being flexible in your thinking and open to new views and ideas indicates you genuinely seek the best ideas and optimum solutions. Surrounding yourself with other respected leaders and individuals builds respect for you. Respect is often equated with the company that you keep and who you listen to.

In a study by Jack Zenger and Joseph Folkman, their research of more than fifty thousand leaders found that, on average, leaders who ranked at the top ten percent in asking for feedback were rated at the 86th percentile in overall leadership effectiveness (Zenger & Folkman, 2009). To build trust and respect, both parties must be ready for feedback. You cannot be in a reactive state. Try to model a calm, open attitude when receiving feedback. Defensiveness shuts down openness. Just listen and take it in—you can decide if you agree later. Take time to regularly check in with employees and ask them how things are going. Ask specific questions that address your leadership and accept any criticism positively and thoughtfully. Being receptive and open to feedback will encourage more feedback and build respect and confidence in your employees.

Following are some ways to build respect in the workplace:

- Make every effort to be kind and courteous.

- Be polite to avoid interruptions or disturbances.

- Call out disrespectful language or behavior in others and actively address it.

- Your language and tone of voice are important.

- Avoid conversations and gossip that could be regarded as bullying or discriminatory.

- As a leader, you must be willing to admit your mistakes and evolve.

Embrace Diverse Views

You are already well connected to others through your professional and personal interests. Think about the last five people you communicated with in a professional capacity. Are they a diverse group of people with different experiences, or are they all the same type of person with similar experiences?

The best kind of network features people with differing experiences and viewpoints. In a nutshell, don't avoid connecting with people who disagree with you.

 ## KEY STRATEGIES

- Remember that you do not need to be an expert at everything. Finding great collaborators who hold pieces of information you do not have is an efficient way to advance your thoughts and ideas.

- Inviting others into your circle of thought is welcomed and appreciated by the individuals you include. Be inclusive in your invitations and pay attention to your friends' friends, as they have much to share.

- You need the skeptics. It may be uncomfortable, but they are essential to your network. They hold a perspective you may not align with, but remember that they represent part of your audience, so their opinion can help inform your work.

- Everybody needs honest collaborators who will not tell you only what they think you want to hear.

- Seeking counsel and reaching out to others illustrates strength and confidence.

If you want to grow your professional network, connect with people on social media, such as LinkedIn. Comment on their posts, or share your own experiences about the topic on which they posted. Ask a professional you admire for advice or their thoughts on a topic on which you are working. Contact them, highlight common professional topics around your work or areas of expertise, and invite them to partner with you on a volunteer project. When your professional colleague shares their ideas in your meetings, reinforce and validate them, giving full credit to them and then sharing an experience you have had that illustrates their point. Offer some of your resources to assist them with their work. Let them know you're a fan of their work, citing some of the projects you know about and what you liked about them. Share admiration for a mutual friend and invite them into your group.

While having your friends and colleagues as thought partners is a great place to start, the best thought partners are the people who do not always agree with you. Their opposing viewpoints will push you to stretch your thinking and force you to think about the topic from multiple points of view. Do you know someone who consistently has alternative views to your ideas and makes the contrast known to all your colleagues? Are there people who have different thinking styles than you? (Perhaps you are a big-picture planner, while the other person is good at details.) Has somebody challenged some of your thoughts or ideas in meetings? Were you ever enamored of someone who come up with solutions you'd never thought of?

While it may feel uncomfortable to approach people who disagree with you and invite them in as a thought partner, think of it as an opportunity to grow. Asking them to explain more or to share more from their lens may be a tremendous opportunity for you to gain new perspectives.

Occasionally, people ask many questions or even challenge you in group discussions. Your first instinct might be to avoid them and call them skeptics or enemies; instead, attempt to view the situation as an opportunity to grow your thinking. Inviting people with opposing viewpoints to a conversation before large meetings can inform you where participants reside in the thinking and agreement scale. Creating a safe space for people to express their thoughts is essential for collaboration. While you may not always agree with people's ideas, there is value in hearing them. You can validate people's thoughts and opinions without agreeing by saying things such as *I see you're passionate about the project. This project means a lot to you. You've worked hard on this. Tell me more about your ideas. I appreciated hearing your thoughts.*

Before an extensive meeting with an audience, have a one-on-one conversation with the skeptic to review the agenda. This conversation is an opportunity to uncover where sore spots may arise and talk through them before the discussion goes public. This "pregame" could serve as a time to build understanding so that when the meeting takes place, you can bring out more diversity of thought due to the knowledge gained from the skeptic. Echoing some of the skeptic's words can show a sign of further understanding and even demonstrate collegiality. Following are some other ideas for including skeptics.

Communicate the goals and benefits of the project. Doubters often need help understanding the goals and steps to get there. Asking for their thoughts on the subject will help uncover the root of their skepticism. Demonstrate that their views are valuable and encourage their engagement.

Ensure that skeptics receive frequent data and information to track progress. Provide research and case studies that support the project's viability and help them envision success.

Encourage doubters to evaluate the work in a critical fashion. Ask for frequent feedback and include them in the decision-making process. Value their skepticism because it can help improve the project.

Have an Honest Collaborator

It's always good to have an honest collaborator who will tell you the truth. What barriers do they see? Where might gaps in the plan lie? If you have directions or a procedure you would like to test before passing it to a larger audience, these are your "go-to" people to test it out. They will let you know where the gaps reside, where too much or too little information is provided, or what doesn't work in the workflow. It pays to go to your honest collaborators first because they will help you develop a thicker skin and teach you how to listen to and accept feedback.

From an honest collaborator, you can expect the following:

Open communication with a no-holds-barred sense of transparency. They share information honestly and ensure that everyone who needs to know has the information necessary for improvement.

Trustworthiness and integrity. They follow through on what they say they will do, hold fast to their ethical principles, and are committed to the project. They have the trust of the team and stakeholders.

Reliable decision-making. Honest collaborators work to get the best information before contributing to the decision-making process. They respect various perspectives and work to check their own biases and the biases of others for inclusive decisions.

A problem-solving mindset. Honest collaborators will have a mindset for solving problems. They thrive on analyzing situations for root cause issues and are intentional about moving away from conventional thinking to innovation.

Run with Winners

Great leaders know how to get the job done. They know how to motivate and inspire their team. And they spend their time in the company of other great leaders. They watch and learn as other great leaders go about their work, leading, supporting, growing, and evolving as a professional and a person.

One of the key components in becoming a great, effective Edtech Leader is knowing what leadership skills are essential to your leadership learning. You must be cognizant of what leadership skills, techniques, and tools you need to sharpen to improve your leadership. By associating with leaders you admire, you can grow and evolve into the leader you want to be. Warren Buffett said, "It's better to hang out with people better than you. Pick out associates whose behavior is better than yours, and you'll drift in that direction" (2004 Berkshire Hathaway Annual Meeting, 2020).

 KEY STRATEGIES

- Surround yourself with people who challenge you and motivate you.
- Surround yourself with people who share your aspirations and your ambitions.
- Abandon negative relationships.
- Seek out people who are more intelligent than you, more hardworking than you, more visionary than you, and more positive than you.

To be a savvy Edtech Leader, you must build the skills and attributes that define great leaders. By building relationships with successful leaders and monitoring their actions and behaviors, you can learn from the best as you seek to be your best.

Seek to network with and learn from successful leaders who:

- Are good organizers
- Know how to manage time
- Create working environments that emphasize TEAM: Together, Everyone Achieves More

- Are flexible and open to different approaches
- Set realistic goals

The behavior of the colleagues you associate with and learn from will significantly influence how you are regarded as a leader. It's vitally important you associate with the right colleagues—highly successful colleagues—to reach your pinnacle as an Edtech Leader.

12

Shaping Tomorrow's Edtech
Sustainable Leadership through Systems and Succession

As the Edtech Leader in your organization, you wield the power to shape beliefs within your immediate team or department, and, over time, to build the trust and respect needed to extend that influence across the entire organization. Acknowledging that your role is more than task management and "tech," you recognize the importance of clearly communicating your department's core beliefs, mission, and purpose and the need to have processes and procedures in place.

Whenever her team suggested hardware or application changes, former CTO Donna Williamson consistently prioritized one key question to reference the stated purpose of the department: "How will this proposed change impact student learning?" (Will it increase efficiency, effectiveness, stability, security, or engagement?)

Change in edtech is inevitable. You understand the importance of implementing and sustaining a framework and systems that can flexibly adapt to changing needs and challenges. The importance of planning for the future also carries over into succession planning. Considering the demographic landscape outlined recently by CoSN (2024): more than 52% of today's Edtech Leaders are fifty or older, emphasizing the need for a formal succession plan. Yes, this need pertains to your team and your own position! And the need to grow Edtech Leaders for the future does not exist solely within your organization; it's a much broader concern. All successful Edtech Leaders must actively support their colleagues within and outside their organization. Choose to seize any opportunity to leverage your influence and position to make a significant difference in someone else's career.

Whether you find yourself in a new leadership position with a well-established team to win over, or you're a veteran Edtech Leader who needs to replace a key team or department leader quickly, you can navigate these challenges successfully. To quote Jim Collins' wisdom in his book *Good to Great*, "[I]f we get the right people on the bus, the right people in the right seats, and the wrong people off the bus, then we'll figure out how to take it someplace great."

THE ISTE STANDARDS

Chapter 12 relates to the **Equity and Citizenship Advocate Standard (3.1)**, which emphasizes the importance of shaping beliefs within the organization to prioritize student learning outcomes when implementing technology changes. It underscores the need to assess how proposed changes will impact efficiency, effectiveness, stability, security, and engagement, ensuring that technology initiatives contribute to equitable and inclusive learning environments.

The chapter content also underscores the importance of Edtech Leaders continuously developing their skills and engaging in professional learning networks to stay current on emerging technologies and technological innovations. This emphasis on continuous professional learning aligns with the **Connected Learner Standard (3.5)**, which focuses on promoting continuous professional learning for oneself and others.

Build Systems for Success

A brilliant friend told me the story of the development of the ATM. When the devices were first being developed, customers would often leave their cards in the machine and walk away. The incidence of lost cards was very high. With a simple procedural change, the frequency of lost cards was lowered. What was the change? The initial procedure provided the money first; then, the customer was prompted to remove their card. With this order of operations, the customer often received the money and then left, forgetting their card. With the new procedure, the customer was required first to remove their card; then, the money was distributed. Notice that the "reward" of collecting the money resulted from the customer removing their debit card. The customer would not get their money if the card remained in the machine. The story resonates because it illustrates how a straightforward rearrangement in the sequence of steps can raise the level of success tenfold.

In leadership, there are opportunities to influence systems for success. While they may not be as rewarding as getting money from an ATM, building good systems will save the organization time and money.

 KEY STRATEGIES

- Scalable and repeatable systems are essential for consistency in outcomes.

- Work to build sound systems so that your staff can thrive. As a world-renowned management consultant W. Edwards Deming, said, "A bad system will beat a good person every time."

- Solid systems save money, build efficiencies, and are consistent.

- Good systems take many iterations; don't expect perfection the first, second, or even third time.

- Always work to improve the systems you use most frequently.

Are there procedures and systems within your leadership purview that need some sort of repeatable process to ensure higher rates of success? Are there frequent inefficiencies, delays, bottlenecks, or errors? If so, it could be a sign of a large amount of inconsistent manual work. Redundant tasks that must be done frequently are a blinking sign that automation is needed.

As your organization grows, there may be many one-offs that need to be incorporated into the decision-making process, thus slowing down the work. If this complexity hinders productivity, slows the decision-making process, or causes confusion, it may be time to rethink the existing system. Do you see people or teams repeatedly taking different approaches to the same issues? Are there siloed sets of data or procedures that are not iterated with the whole organization? Does this lead to different results when consistency is critical? It may be time to build a system with transparent data sharing. Are there situations where existing processes or procedures could be modified to fit?

Savvy Edtech Leaders can identify shorter and more consistent paths through procedures that take more than one step. They know the first iteration of a revised process may not be final. Identifying factors that increase or decrease efficiencies may take many iterations before finally getting it right.

You may ask: Where do I even begin in coming up with solutions to ongoing problems? In many cases, the employees doing the work can quickly identify one or more breakdowns that have consistently been tripping up your team or department. Is your team impacted by other departments whose processes are inconsistent and cause inefficiencies in your group?

Once upon a time. a department of technology was repeatedly broadsided by school technology purchases. Schools in the district used site-based funds to purchase technology items without the department's support or knowledge. Funds came from PTO donations, booster club donations, Donor's Choose, and other unrestricted funds from the schools.

When items like 3D printers, off-brand laptops, and printers showed up at schools, building leaders expected the district technology team to install, support, and replace them when they wore out. It raised many questions with the department of technology: When that item wears out, who is responsible for replacing it? Who is responsible for teaching the staff how to use the new purchase? Does the item support learning? Is the technology department responsible for installing and supporting those items even when they were not asked to provide input in the selection process? Who is responsible for purchasing consumable items, like 3D printer filament? If the item breaks, who will pay for the repairs or replacement?

The department knew something had to be done to build consistent guidance for both schools and the department staff so that funds could be successfully spent and schools could get the support they needed.

In the past, the results of site-based technology requests had been very inconsistent. The success and longevity of the items purchased depended on who had the funds, who made the request, or who just plowed ahead to acquire the technology.

To put an end to the inconsistency, the department devised a standardized technology acquisition process so that all technology purchases with funds coming from the schools would follow the same set of permissions and vetting. Standard questions included: What would you like to purchase? What is the curricular need for the item? What software will be needed? How will student data be used in the software? Who will be using the item, and who will support the item in the school? Who will provide professional learning around the item? Who will pay for the consumable parts and the replacement? Where will the item be located in the school?

Once all those questions had been answered and the software had been vetted for student data privacy compliance, the item would require the approval of both the curricular and the technology departments. Finally, upon approval, the item would be purchased and implemented. All questions around training, support, funding for consumables, etc., were already resolved and documented using this process. Building this plan took years of development and iteration, but it saved time and money for the schools, and saved the department of technology time by requiring requesters to "begin with the end in mind" and think through every aspect.

As an Edtech Leader you know that there are hundreds of technology requests with independent school funds that take place yearly. By building a process like this, anyone new to the schools or department of technology can easily learn and execute the steps.

Savvy Edtech Leaders learn to recognize opportunities to develop a "recipe" for success. By deconstructing issues to discover the essential indicators of success and constructing favorable conditions to move people toward the goal line, you can create lasting and sustainable systems that could quite possibly remain in use at your place of work longer than you do!

The tale of the department of technology could be the story of any department doing similar work. Following are some steps you can take to help build systems for success: Define clear objectives. What are the goals you are trying to achieve? Create a comprehensive needs analysis. What is working well with the process, and where are the gaps? Are there other needs this system could solve? Standardize the process. Standardization creates consistency and reduces inefficiency.

Embrace emerging technologies. Would automation or cloud computing help a problematic system? Is there a place for artificial intelligence or robotics to help with redundant tasks? Implement integrated systems. Can multiple systems pull data from one repository? How could those disparate systems be combined to reduce time and increase accuracy? Foster collaboration and communication. Are you including multiple perspectives and stakeholders who could be part of the solution? Are you using project management software, conferencing solutions, and an integrated communication tool? Prioritize data management. Base the system on data and make data accessible for the stakeholders. Ensure data privacy and security and implement a data governance team to make data decisions. Have an iterative process. Remember that the first draft of a system will most likely require tweaks. Build a process of iteration with a rapid feedback loop to keep the improvement process ongoing.

Invest in training and development. Remember that the most essential part of your system is the human aspect. Work to provide training and development for your staff. Help them understand the *why* and their part in finding the solution.

Plan a Successful Succession

Myles Munroe, international faith leader, author, teacher, and life coach, tells us that leadership success is measured by the success of your successor, and that success without a successor is failure. Your legacy should not be in buildings, programs, or projects; your legacy must be in people.

Leadership changes can create a sense of uncertainty and even chaos. Planning for your successor's success is essential for ensuring a smooth transition and continuity of service. With proper succession planning, leadership changes can result in a new, thriving organizational environment. Depending on your workplace, your "successor" might be a current employee whom HR has approved to take your position upon your departure, or it might be an outside hire taking your position with overlap in your end date and their start date.

 KEY STRATEGIES

- Develop a thorough job description. Create a detailed job description that outlines the responsibilities and expectations for your role. Be sure to include specific knowledge, skills, and experience required for the position.

- Establish performance metrics. Set clear performance metrics and goals for your successor to achieve. Help them understand what is expected of them, and provide a basis for evaluating their performance.

- Identify key stakeholders affected by the transition, including staff members, administrators, and external partners. Develop a plan to communicate the transition and address any concerns or questions.

- Create a training and development plan. Create a training and development plan for your successor that includes both technical and soft skills training. This will help them build the skills necessary to succeed in their new role.

- Implement a knowledge transfer plan. Develop a plan to transfer knowledge and critical information to your successor. This may include documenting key processes and procedures, providing access to relevant systems and resources, and scheduling regular meetings to discuss ongoing projects and initiatives.

Leaving a Solid Foundation

More generally, preparing for a successor's success involves leaving behind a solid foundation for them to build upon. Preparation could include documenting processes and procedures, creating training materials, and sharing institutional knowledge. It might also involve mentoring or coaching your successor and providing guidance and support as they transition into their new role.

As a Savvy Edtech Leader, preparing for your successor's success would involve several steps, including:

- Documenting processes and procedures

- Creating training materials

- Sharing institutional knowledge

- Mentoring and coaching

- Fostering a positive work environment and culture

By taking these steps, you can ensure that your successor is well-equipped to take on the challenges of being a K–12 technology leader and is positioned for success in their role.

Documenting Process and Procedures

Creating detailed documentation of the systems, procedures, and workflows you have put in place can help ensure that your successor clearly understands how your organization or team operates. When documenting processes and procedures for someone moving into your job, there are several steps you can take to ensure that the information is clear and comprehensive.

Additionally, test the documentation. Have someone unfamiliar with the process or procedure use your documentation to complete the task. Use their feedback to make improvements to the documentation. Review and update the documentation regularly. Processes and procedures may change over time, so it's essential to review the documentation regularly to ensure that it remains accurate and current. By following these steps, you can create clear, comprehensive documentation that will help someone moving into your job to understand and execute the processes and procedures required for the position.

Creating Training Materials

Developing training materials such as videos, manuals, and online courses can help your successor get up to speed quickly and efficiently. These resources should cover everything from basic technical skills to more advanced topics like cybersecurity and data privacy. Creating training materials for your successor helps ensure a smooth transition.

Assess your organization's needs. Determine what information and skills your successor will need to succeed in their role. This can include technical skills, knowledge of policies and procedures, and an understanding of the organizational culture. Identify any available resources. Develop necessary content and ensure it is organized logically.

Review and refine the newly created content. Review the training materials with colleagues and stakeholders to ensure accuracy and completeness. Refine the materials based on feedback. Test the materials. While this will take time and patience, it will support your replacement's success.

Deliver the training. Schedule a convenient time for a training session with your successor and deliver the training materials in person or online. Make sure to allow time for questions and feedback. Finally, follow up. Give your successor time to review and reflect on the materials you provided. Following up with your successor after the training is important to ensure they understand and find the materials helpful. Seek clarification about any additional support they may need. By following these steps, you can create effective training materials to help ensure a smooth transition for your successor.

Sharing Institutional Knowledge

Sharing institutional knowledge, such as best practices, lessons learned, and successful projects, can help your successor build on your accomplishments and avoid potential pitfalls. Sharing this knowledge with your successor is critical to ensure a smooth transition and prevent knowledge gaps. Here are some of the best ways to share institutional knowledge with your successor.

Document all the processes, procedures, and policies in a knowledge management system. This should include information on how to troubleshoot common issues, configure network devices, and manage user accounts. Schedule regular knowledge transfer sessions with your successor to share your experience and insights. This could be through one-on-one meetings, group training sessions, or shadowing opportunities.

Provide access to the appropriate resources. Make sure that your successor has access to all the help they need, such as manuals, guides, and other documentation. Also, provide them access to the network, systems, and tools required to carry out their job responsibilities.

ADDRESSING PERSONNEL ISSUES

Sheryl Abshire shares that building and designing a successful team takes a leader willing to acknowledge and admit mistakes when realizing a team member is not a good fit for the organization.

"One of the most difficult tasks for me, as an Edtech Leader, was to recognize that a member of the team was not performing well. I had to have several difficult conversations with this team member about their performance, emphasizing areas where improvement was needed. Occasionally, despite these discussions and the support provided, this person still was unable to meet the performance standards we required. After thorough consideration and conversations with my leadership team, we made the difficult decision to end their employment with us.

In these instances, sometimes the employee was not surprised, and other times the conversation was not taken well. I always followed HR guidelines and had at least one other person in my office during these difficult conversations. While difficult personnel decisions were never the highlights of my career, they were essential in ensuring that the entire team was successful."

Introduce your successor to key stakeholders, such as school administrators, teachers, and other staff. This will help them understand the organization's goals and how their work contributes to achieving them. Offer ongoing support to your successor as they transition into their role. Encourage them to ask questions,

Mentoring and Coaching

Providing your successor with mentoring and coaching can be a valuable way to help them succeed. This may include sharing your insights, helping them navigate the political landscape of your school or district, and offering advice on how to build relationships with key stakeholders.

It's essential to establish a good working relationship with your successor based on trust and mutual respect. Encourage open communication and create an environment where your successor feels comfortable approaching you with questions or concerns. Take the time to understand your successor's strengths and weaknesses. This will help you tailor your coaching and mentoring to their specific needs.

Work with your successor to establish clear goals and expectations for their role in the department. These goals should be specific, measurable, achievable, relevant, and time-bound (SMART). Provide regular feedback on your successor's performance, both positive and constructive. This will help them improve and grow in their role.

Encourage your successor to pursue professional development opportunities, such as attending conferences, taking courses, or pursuing certifications. This will help them stay current with the latest technologies and trends in the field. Delegate responsibilities to your successor to help them gain hands-on experience and build their skills. Start with smaller tasks and gradually increase the complexity of their responsibilities.

Support Others

The trajectory of former CTO Donna Williamson's career underwent a profound transformation, thanks to the unwavering support she received from her graduate professor and colleague. During Donna's time as a graduate student, Dr. Martha Kay Shaw, her professor, approached her and presented an opportunity for an independent study focused on exploring the potential impact of computers on education. This encounter took place in 1980. Intrigued by the prospect, Donna embarked on an extensive journey of interviews and research, culminating in the creation of a computer literacy curriculum for K–6 students, which was used by many school districts in Alabama.

At the completion of Donna's studies, Dr. Shaw wholeheartedly recommended her as one of the initial five pioneers hired in Alabama as computer teachers and district technology leaders. Fast forward twenty-plus years: while Donna was serving as the CTO in a second district, she received further encouragement, this time from Dr. Sheryl Abshire, a colleague from a different district in another state. Dr. Abshire recognized Donna's potential and urged her to pursue a seat on the board of CoSN, the prestigious organization for Edtech Leaders. What set Dr. Abshire's support apart was her proactive approach. She utilized her extensive network of fellow CTOs to endorse Donna's candidacy and secure their votes.

As a result of Dr. Abshire's advocacy, Donna won the election and became a member of the CoSN board, serving two terms and co-chairing three CoSN conferences. These experiences provided invaluable opportunities for Donna to expand her network of colleagues and engage with thought partners who shared her passion for educational technology. The actions taken by Dr. Abshire and Dr. Shaw serve as shining examples of support and mentorship, which left a lasting impact on Donna's professional journey.

This section will explore strategies Edtech Leaders can use to actively support others inside and outside of their organization.

 ## KEY STRATEGIES

- Promote a culture of collaboration, knowledge sharing, and constructive feedback. Create a space where individuals feel comfortable exchanging ideas, learning from one another, and growing together.

- Recognize and acknowledge the achievements, accomplishments, and contributions of others. These highlights may inspire others to excel.

- Encourage and take action to support colleagues inside and outside of your organization. Promote them publicly and provide networking opportunities.

- Serve as a coach, mentor, thought partner, or sponsor. Offer assistance and guidance to those who seek it.

Promoting a Culture of Collaboration

When you include others in knowledge-sharing opportunities, everyone benefits from the diverse ideas and innovative solutions discussed. Embrace opportunities to connect and collaborate, and promote open dialogue. Practice inclusivity in your words and actions.

Edtech Leaders who support others actively listen to their colleagues' needs and challenges. Lend an empathetic ear, and create an atmosphere where individuals feel heard and valued. When appropriate, provide constructive feedback and advice, helping others overcome challenges and reach their full potential.

Acknowledging Achievements

Publicly acknowledging individuals' accomplishments during team meetings or through organization or department communications creates a sense of pride and motivates others to strive for excellence. In addition, your spotlight on these successes may be the needed catalyst for their career advancement. Celebrate the successes of teams openly and genuinely, fostering a positive and encouraging atmosphere.

Taking Action to Support Colleagues

Take the next step in promoting others inside and outside of your organization. Networking opportunities are invaluable to professional growth. Actively champion team members within their peer group—introduce them to experienced colleagues when you attend the same functions, meetings, or conferences.

Invite these colleagues to work with you on projects that highlight their skill sets. Consider including less-experiences team members on panels or when leading workshops. Their perspectives are often enlightening and connect with those of similar experience in the audience.

Introduce these emerging Edtech Leaders and highlight their achievements to influential leaders who can promote them to leadership positions within professional organizations or within their own organization. Recommend or invite them to participate in high-quality learning opportunities, brainstorming activities, and collaborative groups.

Serving as a Coach, Mentor, or Sponsor

Edtech coaches, mentors, and sponsors can help others succeed in their professional roles or in a specific facet of their role. The saying goes, "A coach talks to you, a mentor talks with you, and a sponsor talks about you."

Create a safe space for the newest Edtech Leaders to ask questions and for constructive criticism to provide skill-building opportunities. Be approachable and open to providing insights and practical advice. These experiences nurture their professional confidence and empower them to lead successfully.

The term *thought partner* refers to a two-way relationship. A thought partner is someone who exchanges ideas with you to solve a complex problem or set of problems, navigate a situation, or think through an idea. A thought partner is someone who can affirm, question, or add to what you're thinking. It is a relationship that encourages the exchange of ideas. It does not imply that one person has superior knowledge or experience. Thought partnerships are beneficial to new and veteran Edtech Leaders.

The past experiences of Edtech Leaders vary greatly. Some have an instructional background; others have a technical or financial background. Some have served in other leadership roles, while others have not. You may need to switch among many roles to support today's Edtech Leaders, especially those new to the role. Your support must consider their past experiences, longevity in the role, and whether they are new to their district or have come up through the ranks. Some may not feel they need a coach or mentor, but everyone can use a good thought partner and sponsor from time to time. Sharing experiences and best practices is a powerful way to support others.

Conclusion

Shaping the Future of Education

As we conclude our journey through the transformative strategies and innovative practices of Edtech Leadership, it's clear that the role of a Savvy Edtech Leader is both challenging and profoundly impactful. In navigating the vibrant and complex terrain of educational technology, we have journeyed through a myriad of strategies that empower Savvy Edtech Leaders to envision and actualize a future where technology and education converge in harmony.

Throughout this book, we've explored various facets of leadership, from harnessing emerging technologies to fostering inclusive learning environments and navigating the complexities of change management. From the initial steps of painting a vivid picture of the future in Chapter 1 to cultivating resilience and respect in Chapter 11, each chapter has contributed unique threads to the fabric of savvy Edtech Leadership. We've learned that elevating one's career requires a synthesis of serving others, investing in the community, and persisting.

Leadership, especially in the dynamic field of edtech, demands the ability to adapt and innovate, and the foresight to prepare for the future through thoughtful succession planning, as discussed in Chapter 12. It calls for a leader who can inspire and empower their team and model success and integrity.

Your role as an Edtech Leader is not just a job; it's a mission. You have the power to shape the technological landscape of education and the way learning unfolds within your institution. This is a significant responsibility, one that should be embraced with enthusiasm and a commitment to continuous learning and adaptation.

Remember, the path of leadership is not linear. It is filled with both opportunities and obstacles. You, as a Savvy Edtech Leader, are equipped with the resilience and adaptability to navigate these challenges. By staying true to your values, keeping abreast of technological advancements, and placing the educational needs of students at the heart of your decisions, you will not only enhance your career but also make a lasting impact in the field of education.

As you progress, carry the insights and inspirations from each chapter. Continue to challenge yourself, question the status quo, and seek new ways to lead and learn. The future of education is in your capable hands, and you are equipped to lead the charge toward a more innovative, inclusive, and inspiring educational landscape.

References

2004 Berkshire Hathaway Annual Meeting (Full Version). (2020, November 4). [Video.] YouTube. https://www.youtube.com/watch?v=aCke4ICvGiQ&t=17623s

Adler, A. (1927). The feeling of inferiority and the striving for recognition. *Proceedings of the Royal Society of Medicine, 20*(12), 1881–6. https://doi.org/10.1177/00359157270200124

Allen, J., Root, J., & Schwedel, A. (2017, April 12). *The firm of the future.* Bain & Company.

Bailey, E. R., Matz, S. C., Youyou, W., et al. (2020). Authentic self-expression on social media is associated with greater subjective well-being. *Nature Communications*, 11, 4889. https://doi.org/10.1038/s41467-020-18539-w

Barley, S., Bechky, B., & Milliken, F. (2017). The changing nature of work: Careers, identities, and work lives in the 21st century. *Academy of Management Discoveries, 3*(2).

Barlow, C. (2020). *Storytelling: Master the art of telling a great story for purposes of public speaking, social media branding, building trust, and marketing your personal brand.*

Brown, B. (2018). *Dare to lead: Brave work. Tough conversations. Whole hearts.* Random House.

Brykman, K. M. & King, D. D. (2021). A resource model of team resilience capacity and learning. *Group & Organization Management, 46*(4), 737–72. https://doi.org/10.1177/10596011211018008

Caves, L. (2018). Lifelong learners influencing organizational change. *Studies in Business and Economics, 13*(1), 21–8.

Clance, P. R. & Imes, S. A. (1978). The impostor phenomenon in high achieving women: Dynamics and therapeutic intervention. *Psychotherapy: Theory, Research & Practice, 15*(3), 241–7.

Collins, J. (2001). Good to great: *Why some companies make the leap ... and others don't.* Harper Business.

CoSN. (2024). *State of edtech district leadership.*

Cybersecurity remains K–12 edtech leaders' no. 1 priority in 2023 (2023, May 22). CoSN.

Deloitte. (2022, May 24). *The Deloitte Global 2022 Gen Z and Millennial Survey.*

Deming, W. E. (1993, February). Deming Four Day Seminar, Phoenix, Arizona. [Notes of Mike Stoecklein].

Dias, J., & Hamill, J. (2023, July 19). *What is allyship? Your questions answered.* Center for Creative Leadership.

Fromet, J. (2023, May 15). Naval Ravikant: 11 rules for life (Genius rules). *The Little Almanack.*

Gordon, J., & Fleck, P. J. (2021a). *Row the boat: A never-give-up approach to lead with enthusiasm and optimism and improve your team and culture.* Wiley.

Gura, M. (2018). *The edtech advocate's guide to leading change in schools.* ISTE.

Ibarra, H. & Hunter, M. (2007 January). How leaders create and use networks. *Harvard Business Review.*

Kossek, E. (2016). Managing work–life boundaries in the digital age. *Organizational Dynamics, 45*(3), 258–270.

Longenecker, C., & Insch, G. (2018). Senior leaders' strategic role in leadership development. *Strategic HR Review, 17*(3), 143–149.

Lupu, I., & Ruiz-Castro, M. (2021, January 29). Work–life balance is a cycle, not an achievement. *Harvard Business Review.*

Lynch, M. (2023, September 18). *Great education leaders are transparent.* The Tech Edvocate.

Mankins, M., Garton, E., & Schwartz, D. (2021). Future-proofing your organization. *Harvard Business Review.*

Maxwell, J (2022). *The 21 irrefutable laws of leadership: Follow them and people will follow you.* HarperCollins Leadership.

McCaig, A. (2021, June 10). *Leaders who embrace on-job learning and listen to employees have more resilient teams.* Rice University. https://news2.rice .edu/2021/06/10/leaders-who-embrace-on-job-learning-and-listen-to-employees-have-more-resilient-teams-research-shows

Mejia, Z. (2018, September 6). Meet the changemakers in Nike's controversial new "Just Do It" campaign. CNBC.

Miller, D. (2017). *Building a StoryBrand: Clarify your message so customers will listen.* HarperCollins.

Munroe, M. (2011). *Passing it on: Growing your future leaders.* FaithWords.

NIST (n.d.). Balrdrige Performance Excellence Program.

Owolabi, D (2020). *Authentic leadership: How to lead with nothing to hide, nothing to prove, & nothing to lose.* Authentic Leadership.

Paul, R., & Elder, L. (2014). *Critical thinking: Tools for taking charge of your personal and professional life.* Pearson Education.

Reyes, E. F. & Popoff, E. 2023 state edtech trends report. SETDA.

Reynolds, S., & Dhawan, M. S. (2022, September 1). *How the rapid adoption of Edtech is changing K–12.* EY–US.

Stejskal, T. (2023). *The 5 practices of highly resilient people: Why some flourish when others fold.* Hachette Go.

Uzzi, B., & Dunlap, S. (2012, May). Make your enemies your allies. *Harvard Business Review.*

Vaynerchuk, G. (2021, May 28). *15 tips on how to brand yourself online.* Gary Vaynerchuk Blog.

Weinberger, D. (2014). *Too big to know: Rethinking knowledge now that the facts aren't the facts, experts are everywhere.* Basic Books.

Wharton, E. (1902). *Vesalius in Zante.* From the series Great Ideas of Western Man.

Wharton Executive Education. (2020, April). Today, we need leaders who create leaders. *Wharton@Work.*

Wilding, M. (2022). Trusting your gut is the greatest gift you can give yourself. *Harvard Business Review.*

Willyerd, K., Mistick, B., & Grenny, J. (2016). *Stretch: How to future-proof yourself for tomorrow's workplace.* John Wiley & Sons.

Yamak, O. U., & Eyupoglu, S. Z. (2021, January 29). Authentic leadership and service innovative behavior: Mediating role of proactive personality. *SAGE Journals, 11*(1).

Zenger, J., & Folkman, J. (2009). *The extraordinary leader: Turning good managers into great leaders*, 2nd edition. McGraw-Hill.

Index